Problem Regions of Europe
General Editor: **D. I. Scargill**

London: Metropolis and Region

John M. Hall

Oxford University Press 1976

Oxford University Press, Walton Street, Oxford OX2 6DP

Oxford London Glasgow New York
Toronto Melbourne Wellington Cape Town
Ibadan Nairobi Dar es Salaam Lusaka Addis Ababa
Kuala Lumpur Singapore Jakarta Hong Kong Tokyo
Delhi Bombay Calcutta Madras Karachi

The author wishes to thank Don Shewan, Department of Geography, Queen Mary College (University of London), for drawing all the Figures, and the staff in several departments of the Greater London Council and the Department of the Environment for supplying information.
Figs. 3, 4, 5, 6, 12, 13, 14, and 17 are abstracted from source material published by the Greater London Council; Fig. 7 is based on Figs. 1 and 8 in *The Future of London's Past* (Rescue Publications, Worcester, 1973), and Fig. 16 is adapted from *Built Environment*, July 1973, p. 393.

Printed in Great Britain
at the University Press, Oxford
by Vivian Ridler, Printer to the University

Editor's Preface

Great economic and social changes have taken place in Europe in recent years. The agricultural workforce in the west was halved, for example, during the 1950s and 1960s. This unprecedented flight from the land has made possible some much-needed reorganization of farm holdings but it has also created problems, not least that of finding uses for land in the highlands and elsewhere where it is no longer profitable to farm. Closely related is the difficulty of maintaining services to a much diminished rural population or of providing new kinds of services for the holidaymakers who increasingly buy up rural properties.

Contraction of the labour force has also taken place in many traditional industries. The coal-mining industry alone has shed two-thirds of its workforce since 1950. The resulting problems have been especially serious in those mining or manufacturing districts which have a high level of dependence on a single source of employment—a not uncommon result of Europe's industrial past—and the efforts of those who seek to attract new industries are often thwarted by a legacy of pollution, bad housing, and soured labour relations.

Quite a different set of problems has arisen in the great cities of Europe such as London and Paris and in the conurbations of closely linked cities well exemplified by Randstad Holland. Here are problems due to growth brought about by the expansion of consumer-orientated manufacturing and still more by the massive increase in office jobs which proliferate in 'down-town' business districts. The problems are economic, social and political, and they include the effects of congestion, of soaring land values, of the increasing divorce of place of residence from place of work, and of the difficulty of planning a metropolitan region that may be shared between many independent-minded local authorities.

The problems resulting from change are not passing ones; indeed they exhibit a persistence that amply justifies their study on an areal basis. Hence the *Problem Regions of Europe* series. The volumes in the series have all been written by geographers who, by the nature of their discipline, can take a broadly based approach to description and analysis. Geographers in the past have been reluctant to base their studies on problem regions since the problem was often of a temporary nature, less enduring than the 'personality' of the region but the magnitude of present-day problems has even resulted in the suggestion that regions should be defined in terms of the problems that confront them.

Certain themes emerge clearly when the basis of the problem is examined: the effects of a harsh environment, of remoteness and of political division, as well as of industrial decay or urban congestion. But these have not been examined in isolation and the studies that make up the series have been carefully chosen in order that useful comparisons can be made. Thus, for example, both the Mezzogiorno and Andalusia have to contend with the problems of Mediterranean drought, wind, and flood, but the precise nature of these and other problems, as well as man's response to them, differs in the two regions. Similarly, the response to economic change is not the same in North-East England as in North Rhine-Westphalia, nor the response to social pressures the same in Paris as in the Randstad.

The efforts which individual governments have made to grapple with their problems provides a basis for critical assessment in each of the volumes. For too long, solutions were sought that were piecemeal and short-term. Our own Development Areas in Britain provide a good illustration of this kind of policy. Of late, however, European governments have shown an increasing awareness of the need to undertake planning on a regional basis. The success or otherwise of such regional policies is fully explored in the individual *Problem Region* volumes.

When it was first planned the *Problem Region* series was thought of as useful only to the sixth-form student of geography. As it has developed it has become clear that the authors—all specialists in the geography of the areas concerned—have contributed studies that will be useful, not only for sixth-form work, but as a basis for the more detailed investigations undertaken by advanced students, both of geography and of European studies in general.

D.I.S.

St. Edmund Hall, Oxford

Contents

1 Perceiving Regions and Problems

London and the South East region, a *problem*? To suggest so might appear foolish to anyone living in the other parts of Britain covered in this series: North East England, Northern Ireland, and Scotland's Highlands and Islands have all experienced lower than average incomes, higher than average emigration, and economic stagnation in recent years. Meanwhile, as Fig. 1 shows, London remains vibrant; incomes are higher than average, and whatever redundancies take place are often less well publicized than critical labour shortages for bus and train drivers, typists, and postmen.

The hypothetical Geordie, Ulsterman, or Scot might come to London for a holiday and admit after the stay that the rush-hour congestion and noise, and the higher costs for hotel rooms and West End entertainment, do constitute a 'problem'. If he strayed from the tourist's London bounded by Hampton Court, Regent's Park, the Tower of London, and Greenwich, he might have seen house agents' windows in the suburbs, displaying advertisements showing that a house in London would cost twice as much as he would pay at home. In wandering about he might have seen Victorian tenement blocks behind the theatres or have sensed that overcrowding in parts of Westminster can be as disgraceful and degrading as in the inner parts of 'industrial cities' away from the metropolis.

Would he live in London? Would he earn enough to enjoy the orchestras, theatres, and cosmopolitan kaleidoscope in the streets, or have energy enough to enjoy the metropolitan attractions after commuting every workday; would he find reasonable housing and schooling? These questions are posed deliberately because, historically, London has grown by immigration, from both Britain and overseas, of people who saw it as a city of opportunities. But, increasingly, large cities like London are thought by many to be less attractive than smaller settlements because of the costs and effort of living and moving in proximity to, in London's case, over 7 million other people. Dr. Johnson was wrong: a man tired of London is not tired of life in total, simply of *metropolitan* life in a city encumbered by its past, in which the tempo and rewards of life are different from those elsewhere.

Fig. 1. Measures of regional prosperity in Britain

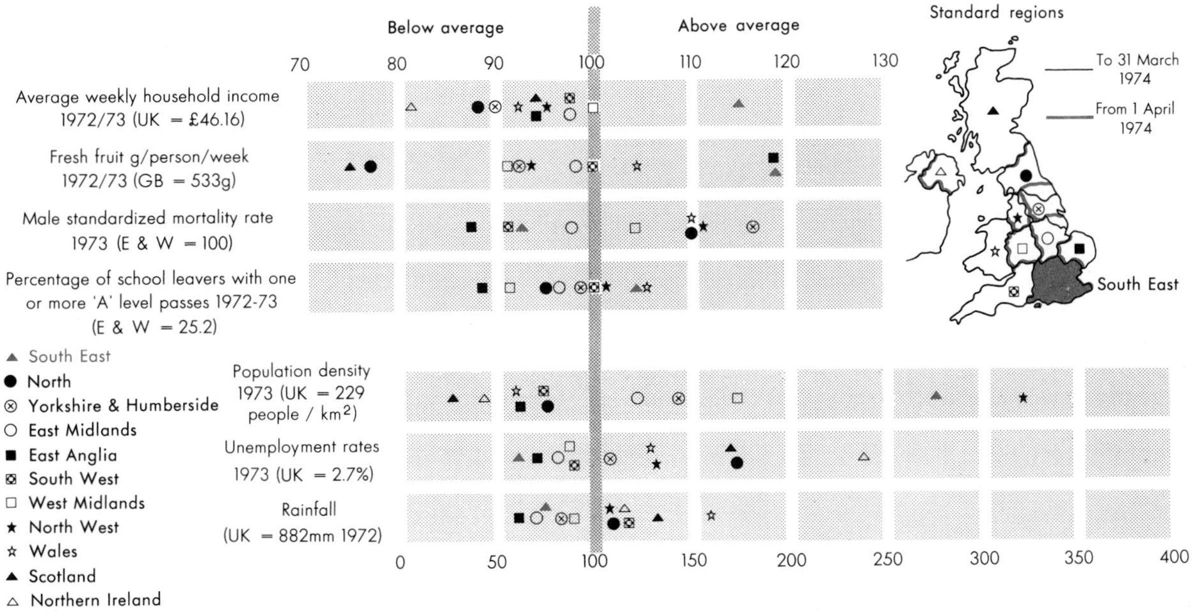

(The value for each region is derived by dividing the regional average by the national average; the national average equals 100 on each scale)

Problems at three scales

An understanding of London's problems can be developed by sorting them into three geographical scales of analysis: local (relating to the built-up area of London), regional (affecting the South East region with London at its core, as shown in Fig. 2), and national.

Local problems. At the local scale of analysis, the geographer still sees Le Play's trilogy of folk, place, and work as the determinants of spatial activity patterns. How are places of residence located with respect to places of work, shopping, education, and recreation? What are the pressures for change in the stock of housing, jobs, and transport networks? How does local government and private business sense and direct change and raise money to improve living conditions? Such considerations establish the quality of life as perceived by London's residents, commuters from beyond its physical edges, and visitors from all over the world. Reactions to London range from 'Flower of cities all. Gem of all joy, jasper of jocunditie' (William Dunbar on a visit from Scotland in the early sixteenth century), to 'Hell is a city much like London—a populous and smoky city' (Percy Bysshe Shelley, 1792–1822).

Regional problems. Greater London's outward growth is now checked by a tightly drawn Green Belt. Because most of London is built over, space for expanding the number of houses, workplaces, roads, and parks within its boundary is severely restricted. Into which parts of South East England, then, should London and the region's industrial, commercial, and population growth be steered? How can roads, ports, and airports be developed for the benefit of the region as a whole?

National problems. London was once the commercial, cultural, and diplomatic centre of a far-flung empire, and many of its best-known features date from the century between Waterloo and the First World War. With the empire's fading, London has retained many of its functions as an international crossroads, and has not become a 'thwarted world city' in this century as have Berlin and Vienna. Certainly, London's symbolic attraction as a major world city and as the nation's capital is maintained almost undimmed. Some even see the United Kingdom's accession to the Treaty of Rome as a new impetus for London to outshine mainland capital-city rivals such as Paris and Brussels. Then feelings of embarrassment follow: should London continue to dominate as the pre-eminent centre in the United Kingdom for government and international business, cultural facilities, broadcasting, and the press? Is the price for feeding London's appetite for symbols of national or international prestige the starvation of other parts of the nation? Such sentiments are not new. An elder statesman at the time of James I observed that it was no good thing for a body (the state) to have a fat head (London) and lean members (the provinces)—a case of economic and cultural rickets.

It must not be thought, however, that London is entirely overwhelmed by 'problems'. Its planners and developers often translate 'problems' into 'opportunities' for restructuring and redesigning parts of the metropolis. Of course many of London's problems or opportunities span all three of the geographical scales, and in practice it is difficult to disentangle local from regional or regional from national. Nor must we assume that London's problems can be solved or ameliorated solely by changes to the built environment. In looking at the geography of the metropolis it must be remembered that spatial arrangements are a product of social and economic status. So social attitudes and political priorities may need changing to ensure that improvements to the quality of life are shared by all Londoners and not just those presently favoured by good locality, high mobility, and the financial ability to enjoy everything that London can afford—which according to Dr. Johnson *is* everything!

London's dimensions

London defies simple geographical definition. In his poem 'The Buried City', G. K. Chesterton wrote:

> And somewhere men without the wall, beneath the wood, without the wall,
> Had found the place where London ends and England can begin.

For C. B. Fawcett, writing in 1919, London's influence, or what Fawcett called London's extended suburbs, stretched from Cromer to Bournemouth. Other writers have assumed that London's dynamism and life-style irradiates all of the Home Counties (Middlesex, Hertfordshire, Essex, Kent, and Surrey and, to a lesser extent, Berkshire and Buckinghamshire). Examining the influence of London as a place of work, we notice that there is hardly any local authority within 70 km of central London which does not export at least 5 per cent of its working residents to London.

Greater London *is* London for the practical purposes of local government and recording statistics. London's government handles a budget

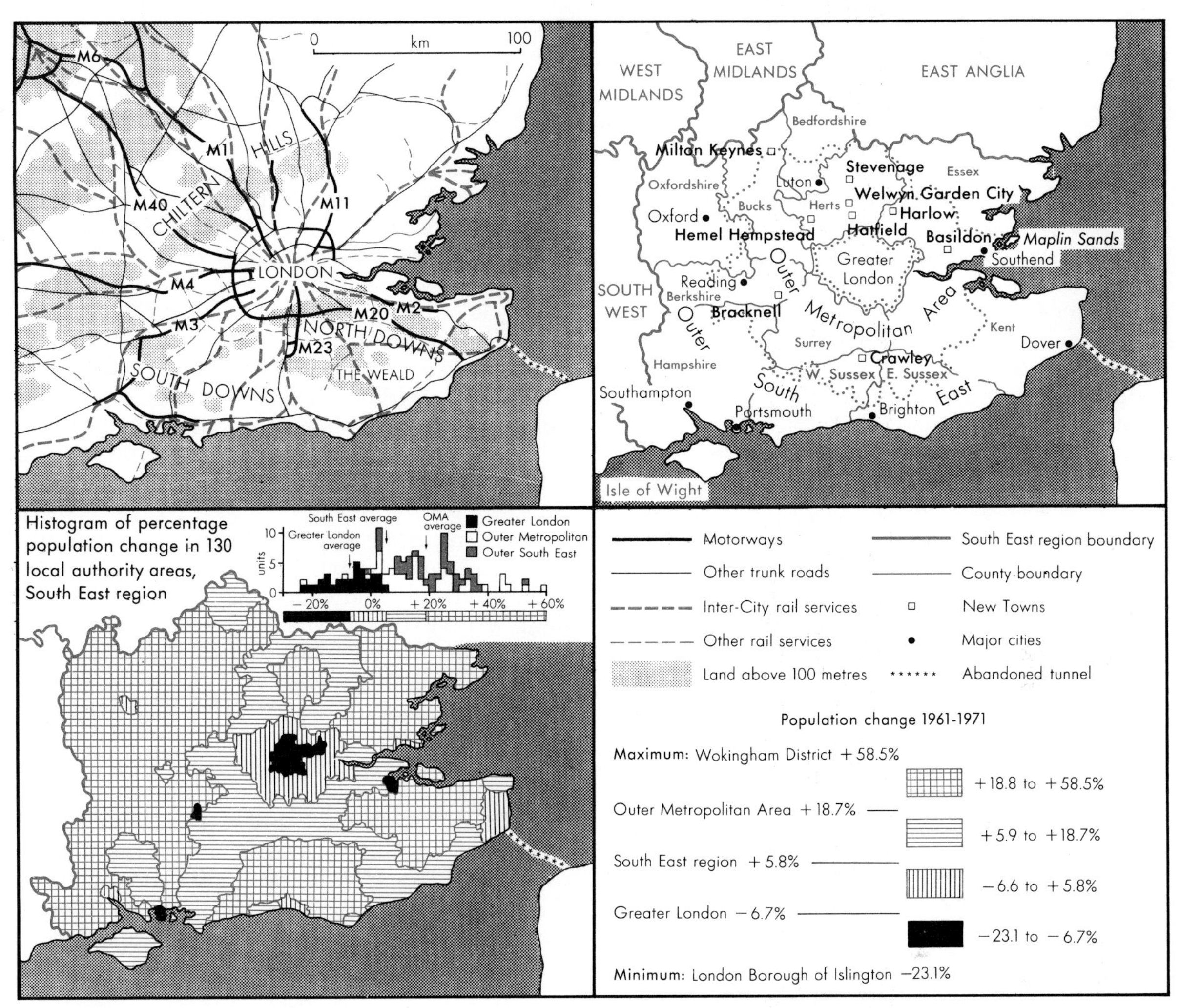

Fig. 2. South East region: communications and relief, administration, and population change, 1961–71, by local authority districts as constituted 1 April 1974

TABLE I

Dimensions of London and the South East region, 1974

	Estimated population		Area (km²)	Density (people/km²)
Greater London	7 167 600		1 580	4536
Inner London		2 830 000	311	9100
(of which: City of London)		(5 300)	3	1767
Outer London		4 337 600	1 269	3418
Outer Metropolitan Area	5 439 100		9 828	553
Outer South East	4 348 100		16 000	272
South East region	16 954 800		27 408	619
Six metropolitan counties in England	11 689 400		6 974	1676
England and Wales	49 195 100		151 126	326

Source: Annual Abstract of Statistics; Registrar-General's *Quarterly Returns for England and Wales.*

which ranks it about level with the eighteenth largest nation state in the United Nations. Since the sixteenth century, when London expanded beyond its Roman and medieval city walls, the administrative boundary of London has been successively pushed outwards in attempting to keep pace with the expansion of the built-up area. The Greater London Council (G.L.C.) area of 1579 km^2 does not quite contain the continuously built-over area. Most of London's Green Belt lies beyond the G.L.C. boundary; the Port of London Authority's navigational jurisdiction over the Thames extends as far as the estuary mouth; the London telecommunications region (numbers prefixed by 01-) is much larger than the G.L.C., as are the working areas of the Metropolitan Police and London Transport. So there are many 'Londons' for different administrative purposes, and it would be impossible to show by a single line on a map 'where London ends and England can begin'.

Fig. 2 shows the South East Economic Planning Region (S.E.E.P.R.) and its statistical subdivisions which are used throughout this book. Since 1965, Greater London itself has been broken down into thirty-three smaller local government units—thirty-two London boroughs ranging alphabetically from Barnet to Westminster (which retains the title 'city'), and at the heart of the metropolis the City itself, the ancient City of London. Table 1 gives the basic statistics about these different areas, and shows how the other metropolitan counties created in England in April 1974 compare with London.

Fixing a moving image

A note of caution prefaces all that follows in this volume. Writing about contemporary London and its possible future structure is like firing at moving ducks (representing major planning projects) on a fairground rifle stall. However, the ducks are not in a straight line; some are moving faster than others and some suddenly disappear without a shot being fired. A third London airport at Maplin recently entered the sights, advanced steadily, and vanished. The first half of the 1970s saw a reawakening of interest in a Channel tunnel: the White City was confidently earmarked as the terminal in inner London—and the tunnel then sank without trace.

This volume has been designed to demonstrate the forces for change in London. The reader will have to correct and update as political control changes in the nation, in Greater London, and in the London boroughs, and, more significantly perhaps, as national economic fortunes wax and wane. With national daily newspapers and broadcasts emanating from the metropolis, it is easier to find out about the changing life and physical structure of London and its region than any other part of Britain.

The reader unfamiliar with the basic pattern of distribution of people within London will find it useful to supplement this volume with one of the atlases of London mentioned in the section on 'Further Work'. For practicality and topicality *A Social Atlas of London* by J. Shepherd, J. Westaway, and T. Lee is a particularly informative adjunct.

Rush hours: the bane of metropolitan man?

London Transport

2 Inherited London

London's future is constrained by the present just as its present is inherited from the past, and in a city as old and complex as London it would be churlish to contemplate possible futures simply by examining its present-day physical structure. Each part of the inherited London of rivers (many now hidden in culverts), streets, buildings, and parks has symbolic and emotional as well as legal and administrative overtones. These need to be borne in mind when any factual analysis of land uses and floorspace, of public and private housing markets, of transport networks and accessibility is being made. But in looking at the inheritance it is evident that owners and developers may not be admirers, and age now brings obsolescence at such a pace that some remnants of London's past are under attack as never before. Yet a glance backwards shows London always oscillating between change and preservation, and constantly straining to get adequate housing, roads, pavements, lighting, and drains for its growing population (Fig. 3), straining to reorganize its government and to balance its housekeeping.

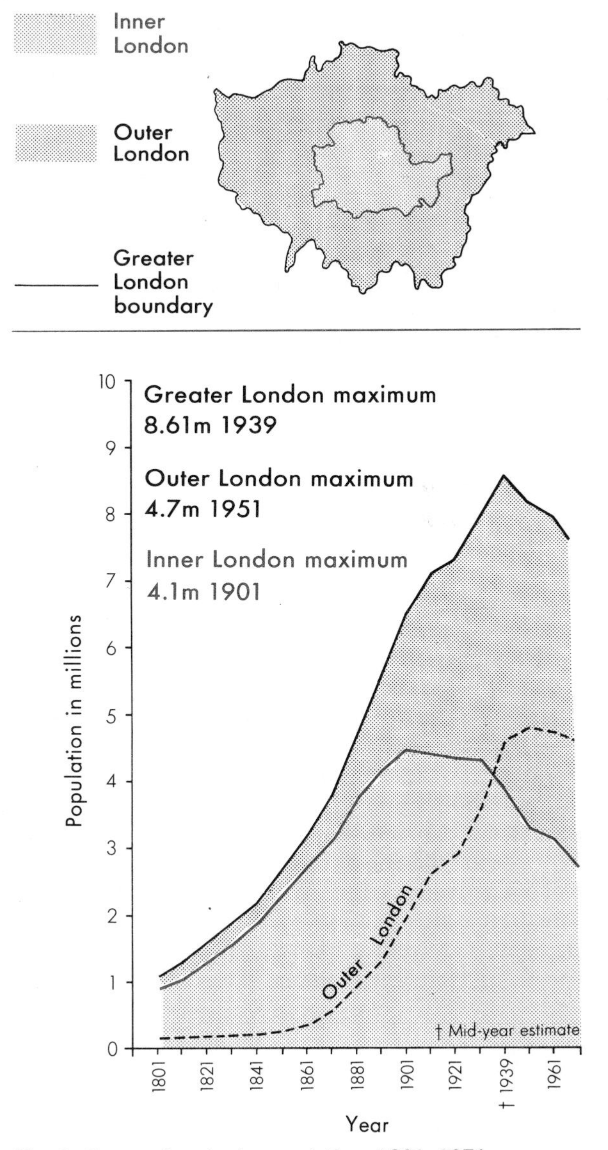

Fig. 3. Greater London's population, 1801–1971

Patterns of growth

City life in sixteenth-century London, which was largely contained within the line of the Roman wall, might have been more flamboyant than country life, but city dwellers were not exempted from disease carried by rats, flies, and drains, or from near-starvation. Maps from Braun and Hogenberg (1574) onwards show London expanding westwards along the Thames from the ancient City—the commercial hub with the river 'hithes' connecting it overseas—and roads such as the Great North Road connecting it to a local 'London Road' in towns throughout the country. West of the City, dominated by the towers of the old St. Paul's and the Tower of London itself, lay the other nucleus of Westminster with the abbey church of St. Peter (better known as Westminster Abbey) and the centre of the monarch's court. These twin nuclei of the Cities of London and Westminster remain the core of tourists' London. Attempts to check the growth of London in Elizabethan times by a *cordon sanitaire* proved abortive, and London grew outwards as it prospered. The population doubled from less than a quarter of a million in 1605 to over half a million in 1690. Riverside villages east of the Tower developed to serve the growing shipborne trade. Urban growth was soon to absorb the spas and pleasure gardens such as Islington and Sydenham which had formerly been separate from the metropolis.

Diarist John Evelyn wrote about one of the consequences of expansion in 1661: 'For when in all other places the aer is most serene and pure,

Art Kutcher

Britain's tallest office building, the 180 m National Westminster Tower, is being built in the City to the designs of R. Seifert and Partners. Art Kutcher writes about it 'serving as a memorial to the aesthetic and economic ideology which produced it . . . and ending . . . 250 years of dominance by Wren's dome [of St. Paul's] over the great visual space of the Thames'

it is here Eclipsed with such a cloud of Sulphur, as the Sun itself, which gives day to all the world besides, is hardly able to penetrate . . . and the weary traveller at many miles distance, sooner smells, than sees the City to which he repairs.' Soon afterwards bubonic plague killed perhaps one Londoner in three who stayed in the city during the morbid year of 1665. In the following year about two-thirds of the City within the walls was destroyed by fire. What an opportunity for sensible reconstruction to the best standards of the day. Geometric plans were conjured up by the minds of Christopher Wren, John Evelyn, and Robert Hooke among others. None was realized, for the existing owners and tenants were loath to vacate their familiar territory. One consequence of the fire is that London has far fewer medieval buildings than, say, York or Chester. But even if his grand design failed, Wren was able to design many of the rebuilt City churches including the new St. Paul's.

By the end of the eighteenth century London had grown to 865 000—second only to the world's first 'millionaire' city of Peking. Growth was not continuous: building booms and slumps are as well described by economic historians as the present-day fluctuations are bemoaned by building society spokesmen. But, over all, London was pre-eminent as the centre of what F. J. Fisher has called 'conspicuous consumption'. Leaders of fashion paraded themselves in London; followers came from the country houses in the provinces to ape them during the winter 'season'. Violent parades also came to the streets as the populace rioted against excise duty, gin, or Popery. The scourge of alcoholism and the bawdy life of the streets was observed and satirized by Hogarth and Rowlandson. All the time London was swelled by immigration.

By 1780 London had four parts: commerce and trade in the City, an overcrowded East End, a developing South Bank, and a fashionable West End in the shadow of Westminster and the Court of St. James. Close scrutiny of a street map of central London will show the West End to be laid out on a grid pattern, but with different orientations to major axes like Woburn Place, Portland Place, and Belgrave Place. The patchwork of grids simply reflects the many separate land holdings—some still intact—of the great landowners of the eighteenth century such as the Dukes of Bedford, Portland, and Westminster (Fig. 4).

In the present century the combination of death duties and the variable fortunes of financial enterprise have allowed a re-sorting of large portions of central London, generally in the direction of the extension of local authority land ownership, and mainly for housing. Some estates have been destroyed, more by attrition than by major assault. The Bedford estate in Bloomsbury has been particularly susceptible to the aggrandizement of the University of London. Others have maintained their eighteenth- or early nineteenth-century appearance, and in the case of the Duke of Westminster's estate have prepared plans for the selective protection of Mayfair and the controlled development of its fringing thoroughfares. Theories of urban economics are of less help to the student of London's private estates than knowledge of the fortunes of inheritance, marriage, and speculation, and, in an earlier period, of the appropriation of church estates and property by the Crown.

Many of the fashionable estates of the West End were on the fringe of London when they were built. In the nineteenth century London burst out of its pedestrian shell, and by the end of the century railways, horse-drawn omnibuses, underground trains, and horse trams made possible the creation of such workingmen's suburbs as Acton and Tottenham. The early omnibuses simply added to the horse-drawn traffic of London's roads; even the underground followed existing road alignments in its cut-and-cover tunnels. But the railways changed the face of London.

Aerofilms

Estates in central London can be discerned from street orientations (compare with Fig. 4). Apart from Victoria Station (bottom centre), the West End has repelled surface railways

Federation by railway

London's first railway ran in 1835, for less than 7 km on 878 brick arches from London Bridge to Greenwich in south London. Thirty years later the scramble was under way by the several regional railway companies to reach St. Paul's at the heart of the City itself. Their attempts were blocked by parliamentary opposition, and London's main-line railway stations still fringe a central area measuring 5 km by 3 km. The suburbanizing influence of the railways was considerable. In 1773 John Noorthouck declared that contiguous London 'may now be said to include two cities [the City and Westminster], one borough [Southwark], and forty-six ancient villages'. Nowadays the 324 railway and 226 underground stations within Greater London either reinforce the earlier nodality of village church and country inn, or avoid hill-tops like Dulwich and Harrow where topography presented a barrier or they were repelled by the trustees of historic estates. If innermost London is a 'confederation of historic communities' (in Lewis Mumford's phrase), the federation of outer London with the centre was brought about by the arch-borne and tunnelling railways of

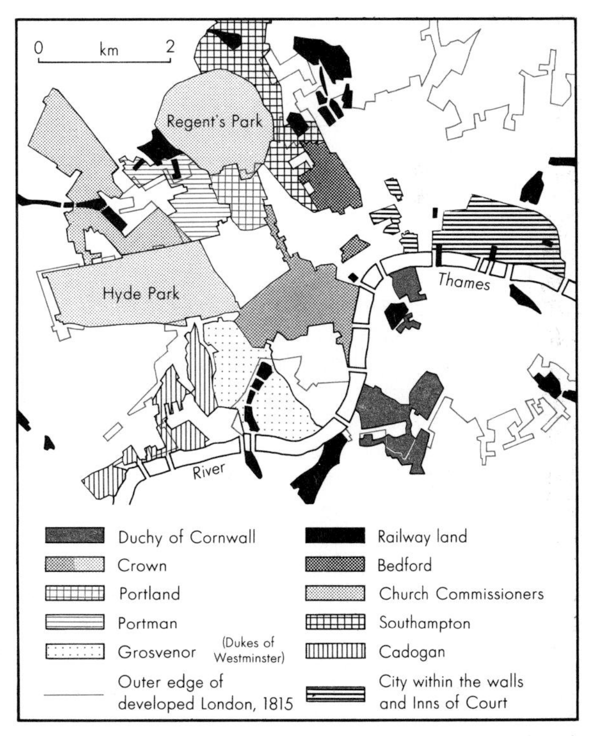

Fig. 4. Great estates of central London at the time of their first significant development

London south of the Thames and by the burrowing underground north of the Thames.

With characteristic vigour, Charles Dickens likened the destruction of Camden Town by the railway advancing to Euston to the 'first shock of a great earthquake' leaving in its wake unnatural hills and accidental ponds. In many ways the motorways proposed for London in 1969 (described in Chapter 4) would have brought similar, temporary, visual disruption to outer London. Better financial compensation for those displaced from their homes, or dispossessed of amenity, is given nowadays by the Land Compensation Act 1973. Furthermore, engineers' designs are required to cause a minimum of delay to existing traffic as construction proceeds.

London growing outwards was serviced by an invisible extension of London under the ground. Asiatic cholera reached Britain in 1831 and ravaged London several times over the next forty years before the 'investigative journalism' (as it would now be called) of Edwin Chadwick, and the five intersecting sewers of Sir Joseph Bazalgette which took London's waste eastwards, controlled the waterborne scourge.

Hazards and nuisances

Other times bring other preoccupations. A combination of the increasing use of natural gas and oil for industrial and domestic heating and the imposition of smoke-control orders since the Clean Air Act 1956 (prompted by the estimated excess of 4000 deaths in the smog of December 1952) means that London is no longer suffocated by palls of sooty and sulphurous smoke. Attention is increasingly given, however, to the emissions of motor vehicles in the incised thoroughfares like Oxford Street, and the G.L.C.'s scientific officer maintains a vigilant nose for traces of photo-chemical smog of the Los Angeles type. He also maintains a roadside ear to monitor trends in traffic noise. The 1970s are not unlike the 1620s, judging by John Taylor's complaint of 1622 that 'This is a rattling, rowling and rumbling age. The world runs on wheels.' It also flies, and much of west London lies directly under the shadow of Heathrow airport flight paths. Even the wider suburbs bear the noisy imprint of stacking zones for queueing planes.

With the construction of the Thames embankments in central London a century ago the river was narrowed and the low-tide mudflats, on which rotting sewage had caused the 'Great Stink' of 1858, were eliminated. Fish are returning to the river, and questions about London's water supply are directed less to the quality of the water than to the volume which can be extracted from the Thames headwaters and its tributaries to satisfy the growing demands of the metropolis in this, Britain's driest quadrant.

The health of the metropolis remains good in terms of the incidence of notifiable diseases, although evidence has been adduced that commuters with several changes of means of transport during their journey to work are more likely to spend time off work than those with a single mode of transport, whether public or private. Non-Londoners might wonder how Londoners survive what appears to be a frenetic and stressful life. But the 'average Londoner' does not spend every day rushing around the centre; indeed, apart from office-bound commuters, Londoners' lives are highly localized in gently pulsating suburbs away from the coruscating core.

Disease and fire apart, one environmental 'hazard' does still haunt central London: flood risk. The Thames could still rise above London's flood defences and inundate 142 km^2, housing 1·2 million people, if high tides, high discharge from winter rains, and north-easterly winds conspired to bottle up the river to the height of the east coast floods of 1953. (The last bad flood in central London was in 1928 when fourteen people were drowned.) A river barrage is now under construction at Woolwich to protect the metropolis against such misfortune.

Imposing order and exposing squalor

When studying London's growth it is useful to try to rearrange the usual assortment of information under various headings. Some are considered in this chapter; others will be found in F. Barker and P. Jackson's illustrated account of London's history (1974). 'Imposing order' implies attempts to adapt London's fragmented government to the size of the growing metropolis, and to extend its legal powers and financial abilities to tackle the problems of administration. One can trace the evolution of the Metropolitan Board of Works, predecessor to the London County Council (L.C.C.) which was, in turn, superseded by the Greater London Council (G.L.C.) as described in Chapter 4. *Ad hoc* bodies ran London's schools, fire service, ambulances, police, asylums, and water supply; yet others were created in more recent times by amalgamation in the docks, public utilities, hospitals, and public transport services.

Under the heading 'exposing squalor' one could catalogue the individuals and pressure groups who have sought to publicize the plight of the outcast poor, to draw attention to persistent

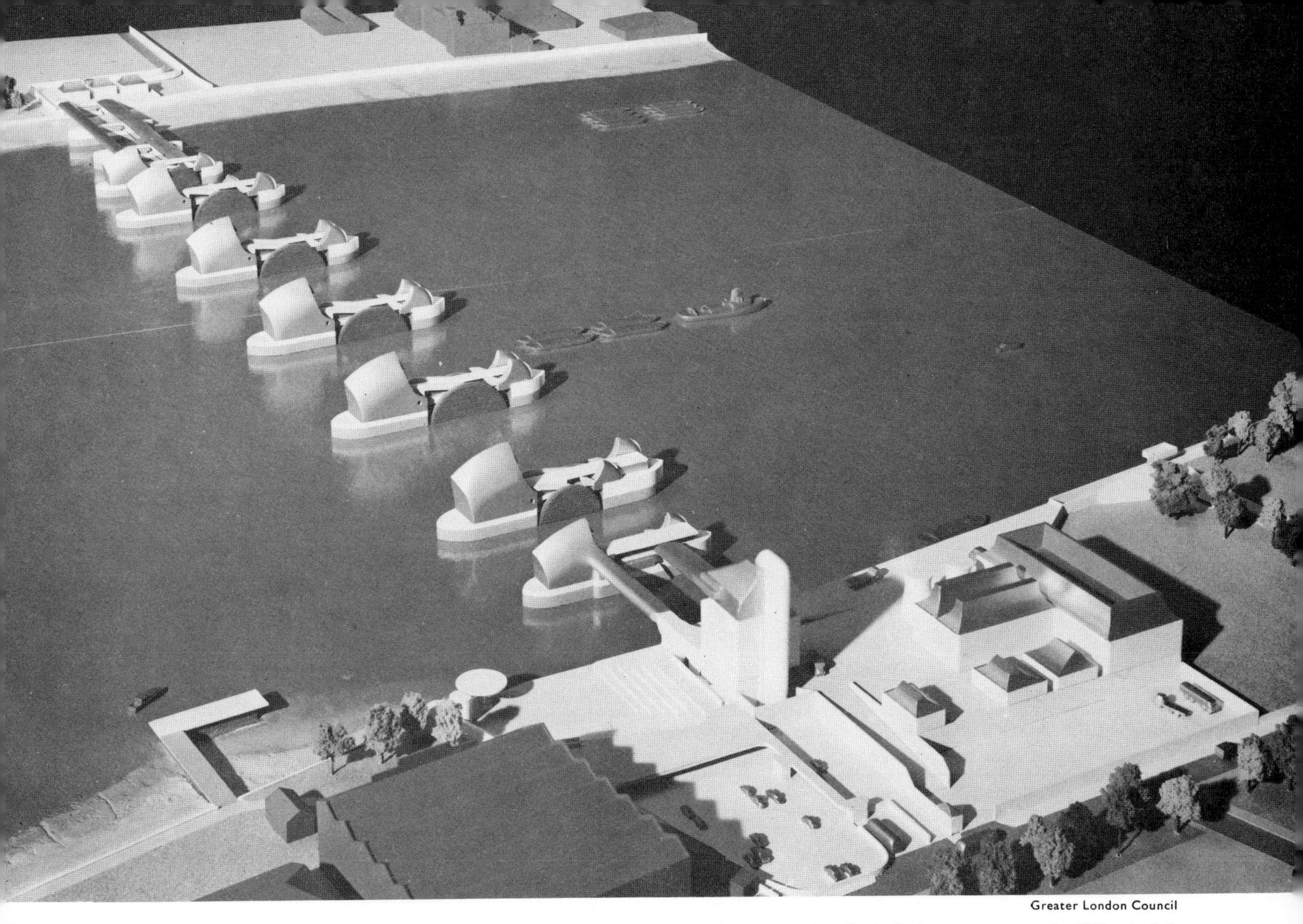

Greater London Council

To prevent the flooding of central London by the River Thames, a rising drum-gate barrier is being constructed at Woolwich

pockets of shameful housing, and to fight against discrimination on racial or religious grounds. As the capital of the nation, London has attracted to it a whole gallery of campaigning authors: titles such as Henry Mayhew's *London Labour and the London Poor* (1851) are particularly well known. Suffice it here to reproduce part of the epitaph to Charles Booth in the crypt of St. Paul's:

> Charles Booth (Born 1840; Died 1916)
> Throughout his life having at heart the welfare
> of his fellow citizens and believing that exact
> knowledge of realities is the foundation of all
> reform he devoted himself to the examination
> and statement of the social industrial and religious
> condition of the people of London. . . .

The gathering of 'exact knowledge' involved a survey of London poverty at the household level, and his resulting *Life and Labour of the People in London* (1892–7; see also the map of poverty in *A Social Atlas of London*, pp. 24–5) is a cornerstone in the empirical tradition of British sociology.

Reconstructing and restructuring

Now that London's outward growth is checked by the Green Belt (described in Chapter 3) and the resident population and workforce is falling, it is faced with the tasks of reconstructing the buildings and reordering the mosaic of land uses and transport routes in the metropolis. In doing this, the inherited London is seen as a liability. Occasionally, unexpected landfalls have appeared on which large-scale redevelopment has taken place: railway goods yards and sidings (Marylebone), airports (Croydon), an ordnance factory proving ground (Thamesmead), and docks (St. Katharine's, with others to follow as outlined in Chapter 5). Supplies of such land are being depleted, however, and London meanwhile undergoes characteristic piecemeal reconstruction.

A larger opportunity for reconstruction was presented during the Second World War when the blitz laid waste more than a third of the City (91 ha during the 1940s compared with 177 ha

Post-war redevelopment of blitzed Stepney Green in east London includes a significant proportion of public open space

Fig. 5. Conception and evolution of the Stepney–Poplar Comprehensive Development Area

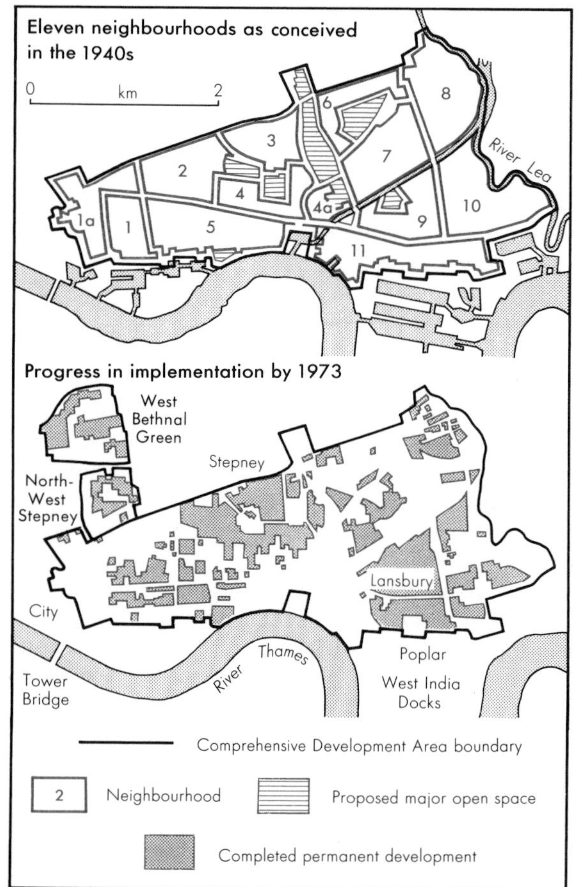

in the Great Fire of 1666) together with large portions of the neighbouring docks, factories, and many dwelling houses. (It must be remembered that London and cities like Coventry, Hull, and Plymouth sustained much less damage than similar cities in Germany; in some ways the post-war building effort in Britain was directed to New Towns rather than old cities, and the sacking of old centres by commercial redevelopment was delayed until the era of the inner ring road and multi-storey car park.)

The City fathers saw once again an opportunity to redesign 'the square mile', and a new plan was commissioned from Dr. Charles Holden and William Holford and accepted by the Court of Common Council (the City's local government) in 1947. But despite major changes to the City skyline, few of the fundamental highway proposals made by Holden and Holford have been implemented. Apart from schemes like the Barbican, the City has been reconstructed without being restructured. Edward Carter's comment is apposite: 'British planning is a graveyard of lovely corpses, each marked by the headstone of a superb volume of architects' and planners' schemes, futurist epitaphs to excite desires but not action.'

Large-scale reconstruction combined with restructuring was advocated for 793 ha of a blitzed and blighted triangle of Stepney and Poplar in east London which had housed 217 000 people on the outbreak of war. Since 1947, 531 ha within the triangle has formed the Stepney-Poplar Comprehensive Development Area which was intended to be rebuilt for 100 000 people by about 1981. Old slums within it have been demolished, non-conforming industries rearranged, and new open spaces introduced. But hopes must be backed by flows of money, and the C.D.A. was only half completed by the mid 1970s as shown in Fig. 5. The Lansbury neighbourhood within the C.D.A. was chosen as the 'Live Architecture' exhibition for the 1951 Festival of Britain, and it has influenced later attempts to build neighbourhoods in the style of urban villages in both New Towns and old cities.

The laudable task of erasing liabilities is not without unwelcome repercussions, especially where friends and neighbours have been almost forcibly parted by the allocation of rebuilt accommodation. There is now a greater awareness by planners, housing administrators, social workers, clergy, and others of the unwelcome effects of compulsory purchase, dispossession, and relocation. To onlookers who imagined that life in cities like London was friendless and fearsome, Michael Young and Peter Willmott's study of *Family and Kinship in East London* (1957) came as a surprising corrective. Slowly evolving, place-bound communities have grown up in the past, but redevelopment has all too often eliminated them in the interests of progress.

Conserving and exhibiting

The sweeping away of archaic buildings and lines of movement is not the whole story. The twin Cities of London and Westminster contain an impressive collection of antiquities including fragments of Roman wall, architectural set-pieces like Trafalgar Square and Regent Street (much altered), and monuments and memorials to Bazalgette and Booth as well as the usual crop of generals, sovereigns, and statesmen. Taken together, these relics of succeeding generations of power—ecclesiastical, crown, commercial, and civic—are the daytime attractions for London's tourists. A survey of visitors to London in the summer of 1973 showed Oxford Street, Regent Street, Trafalgar Square, and Piccadilly Circus as the most widely visited areas, followed by Westminster Abbey, the Tower of London, Buckingham Palace, and the Houses of Parliament. So the legacy can prove an asset, and since the Civic Amenities Act 1967 'conservation areas' can be designated in an attempt to preserve the historic fabric of the city.

Servicing the tourist influx is not without difficulties. Few of the four million tourists entering St. Paul's Cathedral in 1971 realized that it then cost £576 a day to run the church as a public monument. Over four-fifths of the overseas visitors to Britain visit London, mostly in summer. Peaks of congestion occur in place and time: coaches alone converge in the space of a few minutes to deliver 8000 people to watch the changing of the guard at Buckingham Palace. The increasing demand for accommodation has led to the conversion of residential property into hotels in central London, which in turn has led to a search for accommodation for the seasonal influx of hotel workers. In April 1974 the G.L.C., its boroughs, and the English and London Tourist Boards published a plan for the management of tourism in London which suggested ways of levelling out the peaks and managing crowds better at the more popular attractions. Attention is being given to better provision for campers and caravanners and for the 16–24 age group which comprises nearly half of the midsummer visitors.

The new legacy: hotels and offices

In the last two decades, much of the construction industry's machinery and manpower in the London region has been tied up in office building and conversion and, especially since 1969, in hotel building. These glass, steel, and concrete filing-cabinets for typists and tourists have a certain visual similarity. Hotel building in the metropolis received a direct boost through the Development of Tourism Act 1969 which gave a grant of £1000 for each bedroom in approved schemes completed by March 1973. Whereas planning permissions given for hotels totalled 3 ha in 1966, the figure was 35 ha for the year 1971. Individual boroughs approved hotel-building applications without reference to any hotel location strategy. Towards the end of the grant period, as Fig. 6 shows, there was a clear shift in hotel building away from the three central London boroughs of Westminster, Kensington and Chelsea, and Camden (which jointly provided 88 per cent of bedspaces in 1969; one-fifth were in the single postal district of W1) towards Hammersmith, the vicinity of Heathrow airport, and even in Wembley where conference facilities are being added alongside the sports stadium.

Skyscraping, church-dwarfing office blocks covered only 1 per cent of Greater London's land

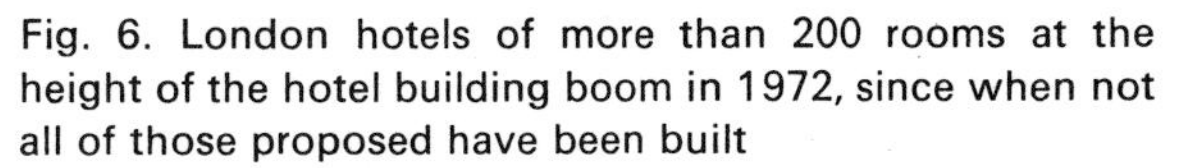
Fig. 6. London hotels of more than 200 rooms at the height of the hotel building boom in 1972, since when not all of those proposed have been built

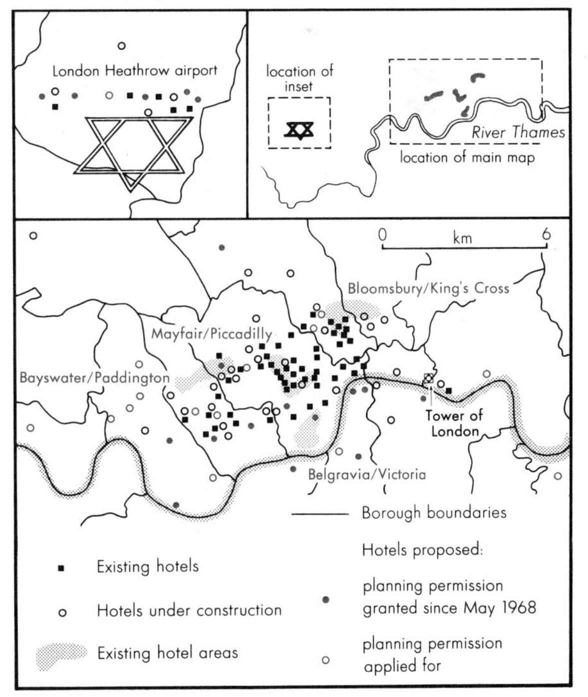

Greater London Council

The Park Tower Hotel, Knightsbridge (left), lies between the West End and Heathrow airport. The Great Eastern Hotel (right), at Liverpool Street Station, was threatened by demolition in 1975

area in 1966, but the figure reached 12 per cent in the 2850 ha of the central area, and 29 per cent in the City's 300 ha. Altogether Greater London contained 28 million m² of office floorspace. As a consequence, 60 per cent of the workers in the central area, which receives an influx of one million commuters daily, are employed in offices compared with 20 per cent in England and Wales as a whole. Government offices account for 13 per cent of the London office space; Westminster alone houses 43 per cent of the government offices in the metropolis.

Fig. 7. War damage, and recent and impending redevelopment in the City of London

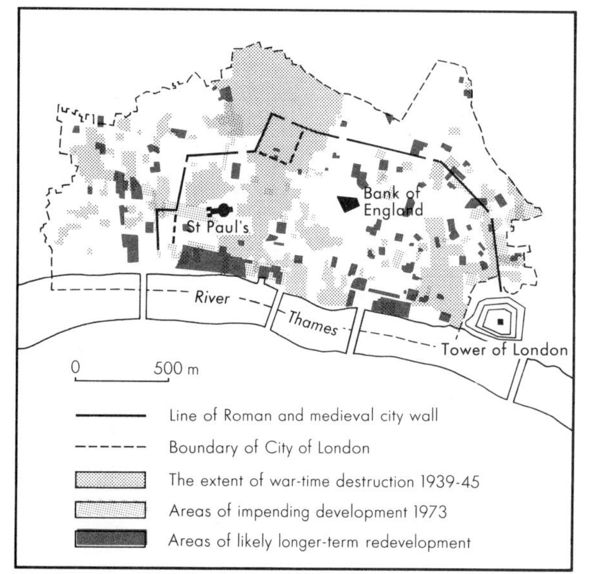

Continuing office building does not necessarily lead to a dramatic increase in the number of office workers in central London. The surveying firm, Richard Ellis, estimated in 1973 that there had been an increase of about 30 per cent in the floorspace per office worker in the previous five years. And of the 950 000 m² of offices being built in the City in June 1973 there was an eventual net gain of only 270 000 m² following the prior demolition of 680 000 m². It is this scale of demolition, together with the scale of profits generated, which fuels the current widespread criticism of office development (Fig. 7). Again it seems that individual boroughs have often sanctioned new blocks with more thought to augmenting their rate income than to traffic, or aesthetic and archaeological consequences. (Tall buildings need deep roots, and, especially in the City, sinking supports destroys fragile traces of Roman and early medieval London, presently hidden by accumulations of up to 12 m of litter from 1900 years of almost continuous habitation.) Nevertheless, attempts are being made to steer office growth away from London, to disperse existing office-based employment, and to decentralize central government functions, as reported in Chapter 6.

3 Problems in the Region

It has long been recognized that London's problems needed to be seen within the context of the Home Counties, the inner parts of which have been touched by London's outward growth in the period to 1939, and the outer parts of which have been drawn into London's enlarged magnetic field for commuting. By way of introduction to the following account of attempts to plan the London region, it must be remembered that individual authors and societies, notably the London Society, have long been pleading for a wider view of the problems of the region.

It was the view of the Unhealthy Areas Committee in 1921 that there should be an inquiry into the kind of authority best able to prepare a plan for the reorganization of London and the Home Counties. Then, in 1929, the Greater London Regional Planning Committee was established by the Minister of Health (there being no separate planning ministry until 1943). It reported in December 1929 on the need for decentralization and the creation of open spaces, and the deleterious effects both of ribbon development along roads and of sporadic building in the countryside. Consideration was given to the need for better control over development, and the Committee recommended that a regional planning authority for London should prepare a master plan to which the schemes of individual local authorities in the Home Counties should conform. The Committee was disbanded in 1932. In 1937 the counties around London joined together to form the Standing Conference on London Regional Planning. In the same year a Royal Commission on the Distribution of the Industrial Population was established to review the causes, consequences, and remedies of the excessive concentration of population in a limited number of large towns and industrial areas of Britain. The Commission's report, popularly named the Barlow Report after its chairman, Sir Montague Barlow, declared in 1940 that 'The continued drift of the industrial population to London and the Home Counties constitutes a social, economic and strategical problem which demands immediate attention.' (About one-third of the population growth of almost four million in Great Britain between 1919 and 1939 was recorded in the Metropolitan Police Area, and about half of all the new factories opened in the period 1934–8 in England chose to locate in the still-expanding London region; the resultant strategic problem was fully evident in the war-time bombings.) Barlow urged that the industrial population be decentralized from the conurbations, and that severe restrictions should be imposed upon further industrial development in London.

Barlow's broad recommendations have been accepted as articles of faith, and they were given substance in the visionary plans of Professor Patrick Abercrombie. Abercrombie towers over the planning literature of the 1940s—considerable in a period of the mid-war anticipation, and post-war realization, of town reconstruction—as co-author with J. H. Forshaw, architect to the London County Council, of the *County of London Plan* (1943) and the *Greater London Plan 1944* (1945).

County of London Plan, 1943

The *County of London Plan* (*C.L.P.*) was prepared at the request of the Minister of Works and Buildings. Forshaw and Abercrombie identified four major defects of the London County Council area (303 km^2, Fig. 8) in the 1940s: traffic congestion, depressed housing, inadequate and maldistributed open spaces, and the inchoate intermingling of houses and industries. A fifth defect, London's ribbon-like sprawl into the suburbanized Home Counties was to be analysed a year later in another report by Abercrombie. The authors took it as axiomatic that the maintenance and development of the community structure of the County of London (population about four million in 1938) should be a primary consideration in any proposals.

In the case of road proposals, this implied that through traffic should by-pass local shopping streets. Throughout, the *C.L.P.* was more a sourcebook of planning ideas than an actual blueprint. Suggestions were made for traffic-free precincts in Bloomsbury, around the Inns of Court, and at a remodelled 'government and commonwealth centre' at Westminster. The proposed road plan for the L.C.C. comprised nine arterial roads radiating from the 'B' ring road (about 6 km radius from Charing Cross). Within central London the main-line railway stations were to be joined by the 'A' ring road, and a 'C'

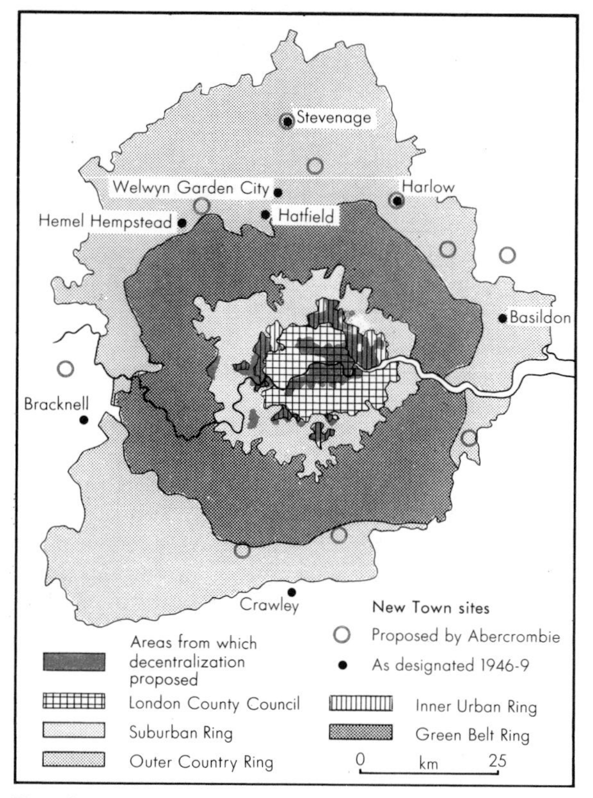

Fig. 8. Decentralization proposals within the *Greater London Plan 1944* region

ring simply upgraded the incomplete North and South Circular Roads of the 1920s. All routes indicated general rather than particular alignments.

Inadequate housing—whether overcrowded, in bad repair, or cheek-by-jowl with industry—was seen as deserving first attention in the replanning of London. In pre-war east London, densities of 450 people per ha were reached; in the isolated case of St. Giles ward, Holborn, the figure rose to 1080. On average about 40 per cent of the population of congested central London, or about 500 000 people, would have to leave for satisfactory reconstruction to take place.

Without the decentralization of many central London industries congestion and overcrowding would persist. Decentralization would also reduce what Forshaw and Abercrombie called 'pendulum travel', the journey to and from work. The authors' treatment of manufacturing industry was full, but they omitted almost completely any reference to commercial employment in their analysis.

Perhaps the most influential chapter of the *C.L.P.* dealt with the reconstruction areas. Such areas had often suffered severe bomb damage in addition to their inherited obsolescence, overcrowding, insanitary condition, lack of open spaces, and inadequate road system. Diagrams showed how the overcrowded areas of east and south London could be remodelled. Three density zones of 500, 340, and 250 persons per hectare (or 240, 190, and 150 net, if communal open space was allowed for) were proposed for areas within, between, and beyond the 'A' and 'B' ring roads respectively. Reconstruction was to take the form of communities, segregated from each other by transport or open space barriers and subdivided into neighbourhood units centred on a junior school, shops, and social centre. Fig. 5 in the previous chapter shows how the model was given substance in Stepney and Poplar.

Greater London Plan 1944

Abercrombie alone was responsible for the *Greater London Plan 1944* (*G.L.P.*). The Standing Conference on London Regional Planning agreed with the Minister of Works that an outline plan and report for Greater London was a necessity. Greater London was defined as an area of 6730 km² outside the London County Council area within about 50 km radius of central London and containing about six and a quarter million people in 1938. Most of the 143 local authorities within that area were already preparing planning schemes independently of their neighbours.

Abercrombie's *G.L.P.* was based on five assumptions, which are listed below (with subsequent history in parentheses).

1. That the ban on new industry in London and the Home Counties recommended by Barlow would be effective. (It was—but for manufacturing, not for office employment.)
2. That 618 000 people within the L.C.C. area, 415 000 from overcrowded places beyond, and many industries, would need to be decentralized from the 'central mass' of London. (The former L.C.C. area lost double that total number of people between 1939 and 1971; manufacturing jobs in Greater London fell from 1 604 000 to 1 201 000 between 1961 and 1971; professional services grew by 20 per cent in the same period to a total of 1 173 000.)
3. That the total population of the area would not increase. (The Outer Metropolitan Area, though not strictly comparable with the *G.L.P.* area, nevertheless increased in population by 53 per cent between 1951 and 1971.)
4. That the Port of London would thrive. (Port

TABLE 2
Anticipated origin and destination of Abercrombie's decentralized London

Origin	
Decentralization from the L.C.C.	618 000
Decentralization from the continuously built-up area beyond L.C.C. boundary	415 000
	1 033 000
Destination	
Decentralization in and near the *Greater London Plan* region	
1. Immediate post-war housing (quasi-satellites of the Becontree type)	125 000
2. Additions to existing towns, mainly in the Outer Country Ring	261 000
3. Eight new satellite towns outside the Green Belt Ring	383 000
Dispersal outside the *Greater London Plan* region	
4. Additions to existing towns outside the *G.L.P.* boundary, mostly 65–80 km from the centre of London	164 000
5. Dispersed wholly beyond metropolitan influence	100 000
	1 033 000

Source: adapted from *Greater London Plan 1944*, 1945.

employment and traffic have been reduced, and upstream docks lie idle.)

5. That new powers for planning would become available, including powers for controlling land values. (Planning powers do exist; bills to control profit on development land have been three times introduced into Parliament and twice repealed since 1947.)

Four rings were identified for analysis (Fig. 8). The Inner Urban Ring represented the extensions of Victorian London beyond the L.C.C.'s 1889 boundary. 'In the Suburban Ring is found the "average man" of the L.C.C. estates who travels 16 miles a day . . .', wrote Abercrombie of this inter-war annulus. Being already built over at a moderate density it could not receive decentralized people or businesses. The next zone, the Green Belt Ring, might have been thought suitable for growth, but Abercrombie demurred: 'A stretch of open country at the immediate edge of the unwieldy mass of building is imperative.' So it was to the fourth ring, the Outer Country Ring, that Abercrombie looked for a series of New Towns limited in number and in size to take most of the tide of decentralization.

The decentralization proposals were related to studies of land availability in existing towns and on vacant sites throughout the Greater London area (the supply side of the housing equation), and the need for reduced densities in the congested centre (the demand side). To the proposed movement of 1 033 000 people, as identified in Table 2, Abercrombie added 234 000 people whose emigration would be 'sporadic or individualistic', so that the total outflow from the congested L.C.C. and Inner Urban Ring would be 1·27 million people.

It needs emphasizing that such a number could not move all at once; the process would be gradual. But the enforced dispersal of people and industries from London, especially when the wave of heavy bombing began, meant that many Londoners were aware of the need for migration, even if they were sceptical of its social benefits. Indeed, many so-called 'Londoners' had migrated to this boom region only in the inter-war period. Few people now realize that Ford at Dagenham relocated from Manchester, bringing 3000 skilled workers (90 per cent of the workforce) in 1928; Slough's growth (from 20 000 to 51 000 between 1921 and 1938) depended on people who came from the depressed areas to work in its expanding consumer industries.

The Green Belt

Had there not been a green belt to contain the metropolis there is little doubt that London would have continued to sprawl outwards after 1945. The still-independent pre-war railway companies had plans to further encourage suburban development when war broke out. The idea of a *cordon sanitaire* to check the outward growth of London is old-established. In the first Elizabethan age the system was abused widely; in the neo-Elizabethan age London's outward extension has been halted most successfully.

At the beginning of the present century a narrow 'green girdle' was proposed for London which would offer recreation and solace in the countryside for Londoners. In 1933 Sir Raymond Unwin proposed a double girdle with two green strands 10 km apart. The L.C.C. approved the girdle concept, and proposed to invest £2 million in 1935 for the preservation of land outside the L.C.C. area boundary as public open space. The surrounding local authorities were to be offered half the cost of purchasing land for the purpose out of the L.C.C.'s fund. The novel scheme was legalized as the Green Belt Act 1938. Meanwhile legal opinion had been hesitant: was it right for the L.C.C. to use its ratepayers' money to pay for activities in other local authorities' areas?

Abercrombie superimposed his vision of a 'gigantic green belt' on the isolated fragments of recreational and amenity land in public ownership. In his 'somewhat tautological Green Belt Ring' he envisaged a strict limitation on the growth of existing towns and villages and a prohibition on new settlements. In 1974 the Metropolitan Green Belt totalled 5729 km² (of which 3080 km² were formally approved, 1818 given interim approval, and 831 formally submitted and awaiting approval), all combining to fulfil the twin functions of checking London's outward expansion and preserving the character and size of existing settlements in the Green Belt.

After Abercrombie

The years towards the end of, and immediately after, the Second World War witnessed a surge of political and administrative energy to build a new Britain. The foundation stones of the Welfare State were laid; gas and electricity supplies were nationalized; and the Town and Country Planning Act 1947 brought the development of land and buildings under a statutory development plan.

Two Acts directly reinforced Abercrombie's proposals. The Distribution of Industry Act 1945 gave the Board of Trade power to control the siting of industry by granting or refusing an Industrial Development Certificate (I.D.C.) to a newly established or expanding firm. In practice I.D.C.s were to be granted freely in the old industrial areas but often withheld in London and the South East. The New Towns Act 1946 led to the designation between November 1946 and June 1949 of eight New Towns to receive London overspill. (They are located on Fig. 8; only Stevenage and Harlow are on sites chosen by Abercrombie, but the satellite principle has been adhered to.)

Table 3 shows that the New Towns now have a combined population total approaching half a million people— significantly higher than Abercrombie's total of 383 000—and the target for individual towns' populations now exceeds 100 000 in some cases, compared with Abercrombie's optimum of about 50 000. Not only are they larger than he envisaged, but their detailed layout has changed considerably since the first master plans were approved in the early 1950s. The town centres, once windswept prairies, now have a welcome air of bustle, and the 1950s houses with spacious gardens have been sur-

TABLE 3

Progress in London's eight New Towns and thirty-two Expanding Towns

New Towns (at Dec. 1974)	Designated area (ha)	Population			Employment		Construction from designation to Dec. 1974 (m²)	
		Original	1974	Target*	Total	Percentage female	Industry	Offices
Basildon	3 165	25 000	84 900	134 000	39 000	42	570 000	34 000
Bracknell	1 336	5 100	41 300	60 000	23 000	37	259 000	94 000
Crawley	2 396	9 100	71 000	85 000	42 100†	39	458 000	43 000
Harlow	2 588	4 500	82 300	(?110 000)	35 200	42	617 000	74 000
Hatfield	947	8 500	26 000	29 000	27 000	33	41 000	3 000
Hemel Hempstead	2 391	21 000	73 000	80 000	36 300	44	389 000	66 000
Stevenage	2 532	6 700	74 800	105 000	37 500	35	329 000	42 000
Welwyn Garden City	1 747	18 500	40 000	50 000	28 000	39	138 000	18 000
Total	17 102	98 400	493 300	c. 650 000	268 100	39	2 801 000	374 000

Expanding Towns receiving overspill from Greater London (at Dec. 1973)	Dwellings for letting (number)		Factories (m²)	
	completed	to be built	completed	under construction
28 current schemes	48 266	90 326	2 843 000	256 000
4 terminated schemes	2 723	—	—	—

* After planned migration has stopped and allowing for natural increase.

† Excludes 9000 at the adjacent Gatwick airport.

Source: Town and Country Planning, 43 (1975), 2 (annual New Towns Special Issue).

Stevenage Development Corporation

Growth industries have forsaken London for spacious New Town sites with good access to the metropolitan market, as at Stevenage

rounded by neighbourhoods with extended garaging and parking spaces for the demands of the 1970s. Although the New Towns are modelled on Ebenezer Howard's principles, as seen at Letchworth (1903) and Welwyn Garden City (1919), they bear marks of individuality, and attract people sectorally from London. Conversations in Basildon shops make the town *sound* like east London in south Essex. London's New Towns have had little difficulty in attracting manufacturing and commercial activity away from the metropolis, and Ray Thomas (1969) has shown that Crawley, Harlow, Hemel Hempstead, and Stevenage, in particular, have a high degree of self-containment as employment centres, in spite of their proximity by rail to central London.

It needs to be emphasized that Abercrombie's population estimates were coloured by the decade of the 1930s. Although there had been a net population increase by migration between 1919 and 1939 of 1 883 000 in the *G.L.P.* area (and a net loss by migration of 626 000 in the L.C.C. area and City of London, mainly into the *G.L.P.* area) the Registrar-General's pre-war forecast of Great Britain's total population in 1970 was only 45 980 000 people, 28 000 fewer than in 1937. Mindful of the national trend in the late 1930s towards zero growth, and accepting the Barlow principle of no additional industrial growth in London, Abercrombie was able to propose solving London's overcrowding within the largely self-contained *G.L.P.* region.

The actual population of Great Britain in 1970 was 55 million—9 million more than the 1937 total. In the 1950s the counties containing London's New Towns, especially Hertfordshire and Essex, experienced the highest population growth rates (3·43 and 2·77 per cent per year, 1951–61). During the 1960s Basingstoke was the fastest-growing town in England and Wales (+7·27 per cent per annum). It is an 'Expanding Town', receiving London overspill under the arrangements of the Town Development Act 1952, which enabled the industrial conurbations to decentralize to existing towns as well as to the New Towns on their mainly virgin sites.

In the context of planning for the metropolitan

region, Abercrombie had recognized and explained the necessity of planning for the City of London, County of London, and Greater London Plan region *as a whole*. In the *G.L.P.* he pressed for the creation of a board which would ensure that future developments conformed to a master plan. It should not just be a sanctioning authority with power only to prevent the wrong use of land, but should also be able to acquire and sell land and construct roads and buildings.

In 1947 an Advisory Committee for London Regional Planning accepted the plan in broad outline, as did the Minister for Town and Country Planning. But in that year counties and county boroughs in England and Wales became 'planning authorities' and were required to prepare development plans showing land zoned for housing, industry, and other uses, over a twenty-year period—the whole to be approved by the Minister, and to be reviewed at five-year intervals to allow for changing circumstances. Accordingly, the six County Councils (London, Middlesex, Hertfordshire, Essex, Kent, and Surrey) and three County Borough Councils (Croydon, East Ham, and West Ham) prepared plans independently. Despite the recommendation of the Clement Davies Committee (1949) for a regional authority with powers of supervision, direction, and finance for the *G.L.P.*, no such body was given the power to co-ordinate Greater London planning. Even when the Local Government Boundary Commission for England was established in 1945, the County of London was excluded from its brief to suggest new boundaries for more effective local government.

Theoretically the nine county plans in the Greater London region could be made to conform by the Minister who had powers of amendment and even rejection. But in practice the County of London's five-year review (submitted March 1960) came only fifteen months behind the approval of Hertfordshire's first (twenty-year) development plan (December 1958). How could the plans be co-ordinated when they each had a different time-horizon?

Towards the end of the 1950s, pressures for a review of London government resulted in the appointment of the Royal Commission on Local Government in Greater London (1957–60), chaired by Sir Edwin Herbert. Although it led to the London Government Act 1963 and the creation of the Greater London Council in 1965 (described in Chapter 4), there was still no public agency to review planning problems throughout Abercrombie's wider *G.L.P.* region.

South East Study, 1964

A White Paper entitled *London—Employment: Housing: Land* (1963) showed that the Government saw the need for a regional plan for London and the South East, and the Ministry of Housing and Local Government's *South East Study* (*S.E.S.*) was published in March 1964. One of its primary aims was to give local planning authorities in South East England a framework within which to set their individual county development plans. In the light of the post-war bulge in births, the Registrar-General projected in 1948 a population of 45 280 000 in England and Wales by 1971, that is an increase of about two million over the period 1951–71. The actual increase was of the order of five million, as shown in Table 4. As Fig. 9 shows, there was a surge in the birth-rate in 1947, and a progressive increase after the secondary nadir of 1955. By the early 1960s the estimated increase in population in England and Wales over the period 1961–81 was six million by natural increase and one million by net immigration—that represents an increase of 350 000 a year overall.

As already stated, Barlow and Abercrombie had both assumed that with a static population nationally and regionally, the task of replanning congested London could be achieved by the decentralization of jobs and people within the South East. Alarm bells sounded in the *S.E.S.* An anticipated gain in the South East of one million migrants and a further two and a half million by natural increase required housing for an extra three and a half million people above the continuing pressures of London overspill. Equally alarming was the recent increase of jobs in the London conurbation—+63 000 annually in the early 1960s—and there was then a current annual increase of +15 000 office jobs in London's central area. Abercrombie had assumed no growth of jobs in London, and the I.D.C. dispersal mechanism related to manufacturing, not

TABLE 4
Population change in England and Wales: projected and actual (in millions)

	1951	1961	1971	1981
Projected				
1948	←	+2	→ 45·28	
early 1960s		←	+7	→
1973		←	+3·5 →	49·57
Actual	43·82	46·20	48·85	

Source: various issues of *Social Trends*.

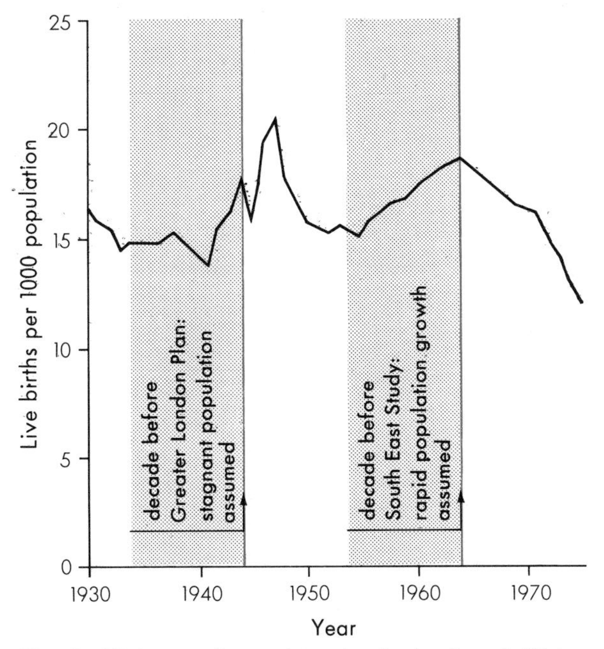

Fig. 9. Birth-rate fluctuations in England and Wales, 1930–75—population trends are the most basic input of regional plans

to the booming office-based service industries. Commuting was increasing, with an additional 20 000 workers a year entering the central area in each of the five years before the *S.E.S.* was published. Work journeys were also lengthening. The Green Belt and continuing shortage of accommodation within built-over London could be blamed for that.

Repeating the need to ensure that as much growth as possible should take place outside the South East, the *S.E.S.* then considered how to distribute the population and employment growth that seemed inevitable, together with the London overspill. Three major new cities were proposed, for Southampton/Portsmouth and for the Bletchley and Newbury areas. Possible New Towns at Ashford and Stansted, shown in Fig. 10, were also discussed. In addition the *S.E.S.* proposed large-scale town expansions, and a further category of extensions to a dozen existing settlements, to accommodate a total of one to one and a quarter million people. The remaining two-thirds of the anticipated growth would have to take place on the land allocated in development plans by planning authorities.

The *S.E.S.* was adamant that office growth in London should not just be halted, but even reversed by decentralization. And as a by-product of the anticipated population growth there was an urgent need to improve water supplies to south-east Essex—the driest corner of Britain.

Then before the end of 1964 the Conservative Government was succeeded by a Labour one. The new Government was committed firmly to planning. A new Department of Economic Affairs established planning councils and boards in eight new economic planning regions in England, including a new, smaller South East region which excluded East Anglia (compare Figs. 10*a* and *b*). Indeed the new Labour Government announced in November 1964 that their first action in the field of comprehensive regional planning was 'designed to check the continued growth of offices in South East England, especially in London, and thus to relieve congestion, and secure a better distribution of employment and a better use of resources'. The desire to control office as well as industrial development brought the Office Development Permit (O.D.P.) system, broadly analogous to the I.D.C. introduced for manufacturing industries in 1945. Since 1964 all proposed office developments exceeding 280 m^2 in the London region have needed an O.D.P. in addition to the usual planning permission. In granting an O.D.P., the Department of the Environment sought evidence that a firm needed a London location. For those firms hesitant about the merits of a London location the Location of Offices Bureau, established in 1962, offered

Cut loose before London office costs squeeze <u>your</u> company to death

Location of Offices Bureau

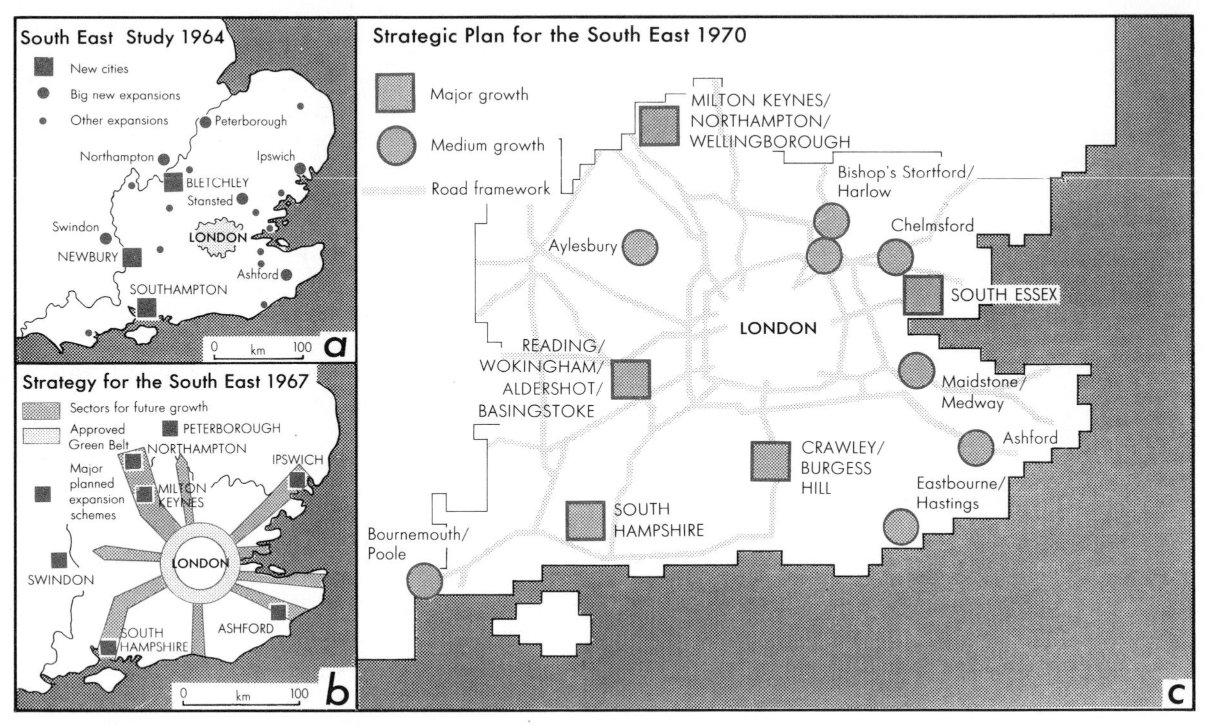

Fig. 10. *Study*, *Strategy*, and *Strategic Plan* for the South East region

ample propaganda on the benefits of moving out of town, and since June 1973 the Department of Trade has offered grants for office-based enterprises to move to the development areas. In 1965 the so-called 'Brown Ban' (after George Brown, then in charge of the new Department of Economic Affairs) hit hard: only 9615 m² of office building was countenanced in Greater London. By 1969 the figure was 177 440 m² (Fig. 11). The ban led to soaring rents for existing premises, and in the 1970s office development has been affected more by interest charges and investment confidence than the O.D.P. system as such.

A Strategy for the South East, 1967

Each regional economic planning council, comprising people prominent in the region's business, politics, and universities, had to prepare a regional review followed by a strategy for development. In the case of the South East, the Government itself had started work on the *S.E.S.* in 1961, and the new planning council moved directly to *A Strategy for the South East* (*S.S.E.*), published in 1967.

'The growth of London must be contained,' stated the *S.S.E.*—still echoing Barlow and Abercrombie. A new method of containing the region's dynamism was proposed: the development of city regions around the periphery of the region in which clusters of towns could act as effective counter-magnets to attract population and industry away from London. Fig. 10*b* shows how the chosen clusters would be located along transport corridors—interestingly, a form of development also favoured for Copenhagen, Paris, Stockholm, and Washington, D.C., in the

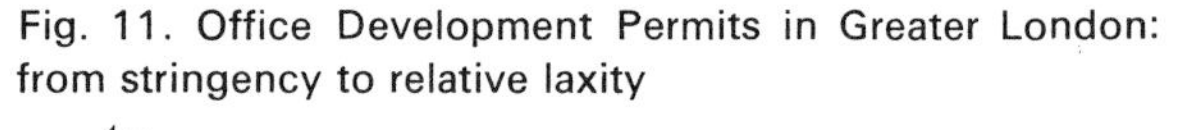
Fig. 11. Office Development Permits in Greater London: from stringency to relative laxity

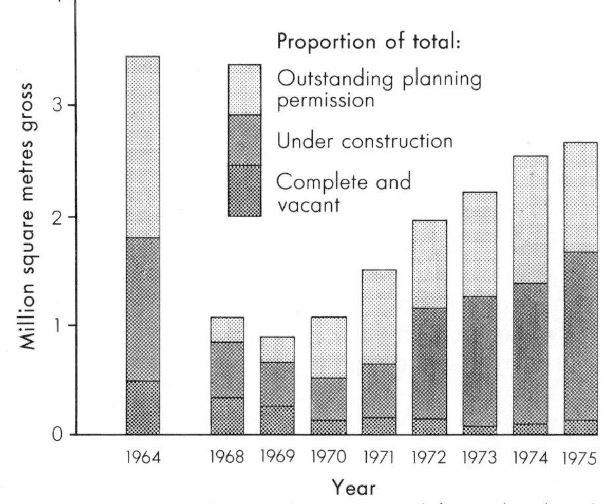

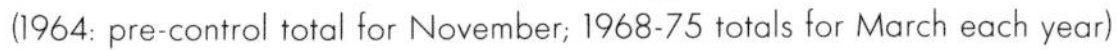
(1964: pre-control total for November; 1968-75 totals for March each year)

mid 1960s. Country zones would act as buffers between the radial spokes.

It is in the *S.S.E.* that we see the emergence of the idea of a slower rate of growth in the South East. For the period 1964–81 the slightly smaller South East region now has a projected growth of 2·14 million, and it is thought that natural increase (the excess of births over deaths) will account for virtually the whole amount. 'The region is likely to lose more people to other parts of England and Wales than it gains from drifts,' stated the *S.S.E.* There are other assumptions which have since been confounded: the council had assumed that the Channel tunnel would be built in the 1970s, for example. Also, by a curious turn of events, Stansted, which was chosen as the site of London's third airport in 1967, is now likely to fulfil that role, having been reprieved between 1968 and 1975, during which period Maplin emerged as the preferred location. Some curious statistical anomalies are revealed in the *S.S.E.* Whereas Greater London's employment growth between 1951 and 1961 was +1·0 per cent per annum, according to the Ministry of Labour statistics used in the *S.E.S.*, the census of population in 1961 revealed a rate of no more than +0·4 per cent.

TABLE 5

Population projections and alternative hypotheses for the South East region and its subdivisions (in thousands)

	Actual population			
	Greater London	Outer Metropolitan Area	Outer South East	South East total
1951	8206	3497	3513	15 216
1961	7977	4504	3865	16 346
1971*	7441	5345	4207	16 993
1972*	7345	5403	4272	17 020
1973*	7281	5423	4314	17 019
1974*	7168	5439	4348	16 955
	Estimated population			
	Strategy for the South East (1967)			
1971	7940	5360	4400	17 690
1981	8010	5900	5060	18 970
	Greater London Development Plan (1969)			
1981	7336 (high) 7123 (low)			
	Strategic Plan for the South East (1970)			
1981	7336	6190	5161	18 687
1991A	7336	6839	5804	20 135†
1991B	7000	7222	5914	20 136
	G.L.C. Research Memorandum No. 455 (1975)			
1981	6541 (high) 6344 (low)			

* Figures not directly comparable with 1951 and 1961 because of changed boundaries.
† Includes 156 000 accommodated outside the region.

Source: Registrar-General's *Quarterly Returns for England and Wales* and the reports cited.

***Strategic Plan for the South East*, 1970**

Although the *S.S.E.* was perceptive and made positive proposals, it found little favour with local authorities in the South East. A Standing Conference on London and South East Regional Planning (S.C.L.S.E.R.P.) had been established in 1962 to review planning issues, establish joint policies, and liaise with relevant government departments. To be accurate, the words 'and South East' were not inserted until 1966 when its boundaries were extended from the London Metropolitan Area to conform with the new economic planning region. Being an advisory document only, the *S.S.E.* found little favour with S.C.L.S.E.R.P. members, the authorities that would have to implement the growth proposals. To solve the impasse, the Government commissioned a new regional study in the summer of 1968 under the leadership of the Ministry of Housing and Local Government's chief planner. The new South East Joint Planning Team consisted of representatives of ministries, S.C.L.S.E.R.P., local authority planners, and consultants, and the third regional policy document for the South East in six years appeared in 1970 entitled *Strategic Plan for the South East* (*S.P.S.E.*).

Planning fashions had changed considerably between 1964 and 1970. Planners now sought to test how far alternative plans satisfied specified objectives or goals. Broad groups of objectives were discerned for the South East:

1. *Economic objectives*: to provide growth centres sufficiently large and compact to function as labour markets but not to pose journey-to-work and congestion problems.
2. *Social objectives*: to provide improved housing, environmental standards, and community

facilities, both generally and more particularly for less privileged inner London residents.

3. *Countryside objectives*: to provide for the greatest possible benefit to be derived from the countryside.

4. *Transport objectives*: to provide the greatest possible ease of movement within the region and the greatest possible net benefits for transport users.

Each broad objective was refined by subdivision, yet the whole had to be welded into a feasible regional strategy. Rapid population growth was still assumed: a total of 17·3 million in the South East in 1969 was expected to reach 21·5 million by 2001. Two physical patterns of growth were developed for the period to 1991 (Table 5). The first, called hypothesis *1991A*, assumed that growth would be directed to large centres at the end of tentacles radiating from the metropolis. This hypothesis simply followed the recommendations of the *S.S.E.* of 1967. The alternative hypothesis, *1991B*, envisaged that more of the growth would be accommodated closer to London.

Making a broad distinction between Greater London, the Outer Metropolitan Area (O.M.A.), and the Outer South East (O.S.E.), the Joint Planning Team then allocated growth among the thirty-three planning units they had defined in the South East. This gave rise to so-called 'areas of opportunity' and 'areas of conflict', and the final preferred strategy incorporated a mixture of *1991A* and *1991B*, as shown in Fig. 10*c*. Five major, and seven medium, growth areas were recommended to 'promote the functional structuring of the South East into city regions relatively independent of London'.

For all the sophistication of mathematical modelling and refining objectives, the method of regional plan-making had changed little since Abercrombie. In the *Greater London Plan 1944* Abercrombie fixed zones for residential, industrial, and commercial land uses, and then fixed population targets for each local authority area. But the team had learnt from post-war experience. The *S.P.S.E.* emphasizes the fact that previous regional plans have demonstrated the impracticability of accurately forecasting the scale and rate of growth (or now decline) of people and jobs for more than a few years ahead. In addition, it is recognized that many important decisions which affect a region's prosperity are made by individuals and firms outside the realms of government and local authorities.

Implementation and monitoring

Taken together with its five supporting volumes of research studies, the *S.P.S.E.* represents a considerable weight of good advice and cogent analysis. But is there any way of ensuring that local authorities prepare their plans to satisfy the objectives of the strategy, which was devised for the good of the region as a whole? The short answer is: No. Just as Abercrombie's Greater London spread over nine county development plans, so the South East region embraces thirteen counties, each of which is preparing, or has prepared, a structure plan. (Since 1968, old-style development plans have been superseded by structure plans—prepared by counties—and interlocking local plans will be prepared by the post-1974 local government district councils.) Although the *S.P.S.E.* was approved by the Government, with only minor modifications in 1971, it is still impossible for central government to force local government to plan for major or medium growth. Not all local authorities are unco-operative, however, and the counties whose boundaries converge on the proposed Reading/Wokingham / Aldershot / Basingstoke major growth area have joined together to undertake a sub-regional study.

But implementing the *S.P.S.E.* may be not just difficult; it may be unnecessary. The anticipated population increases in the South East are no longer likely. It may be surprising to some that the Registrar-General's provisional estimates of the home population showed a *fall* in the South East from 17 020 000 in 1972 to 16 955 000 in 1974 (Table 5).

Such unexpected changes point to the need emphasized by the Joint Planning Team to monitor trends and to keep the *S.P.S.E.* up to date. But even if anticipating the decline of the birth-rate graph is like contemplating an alpine traverse in cloud, the *S.P.S.E.* has made solid progress by linking the problems of inner London to the outer rings of the South East region. Like a medieval city, London has crossed a barrier (its Green Belt rather than a river) to establish settlement beyond its formal boundary. We now turn to the problems of the metropolis itself.

4 Problems in the Metropolis

Looking at Fig. 1, someone who has never visited London—or indeed a tourist whose visit has been spent entirely within the West End and whose journeys have been made exclusively by taxi—might not realize the variations in standard of living and provision of services that persist within London. Consider restaurants as an extreme example. In the City of Westminster, directly west of the City of London, in 1972 there were 733 premises classified exclusively as restaurants for rating purposes; in Tower Hamlets, adjoining the City of London to the east, there were four. In the same year, the borough of Richmond upon Thames (population 170 000) had 1989 ha of public open space; Islington (population 179 000) had 35 ha. In Havering at the time of the 1971 census, only 2 per cent of the population were born outside the British Isles; in ten other London boroughs the figure exceeded 15 per cent. Obviously clusters and local specializations will always be present, but the task of London's government is to redress the grosser inequalities of access to housing, services, and amenities in the metropolis.

Metropolitan reform, 1957–63

The G.L.C., comprising both the elected government and recruited administrators, is the government of London. Greater London, an area of 58 by 46 km (1579 km²), became the new government unit for the metropolis on 1 April 1965, but not without a protracted struggle. Chapter 3 mentions the establishment of the Royal Commission on London Government (1957–60), which recommended the creation of a Council for Greater London and, provisionally, fifty-two Greater London boroughs including the City of London. These proposals were modified, and a reduced G.L.C. area came to consist of thirty-two London boroughs together with the City of London.

At its simplest, opposition to the reform of London government and boundaries was prompted by the London Labour Party's fear that enlarged boundaries would take in Conservative suburbs and so threaten Labour's hold on London. The old London County Council had been Labour-dominated since 1934. Table 6 shows the balance of power in the counties surrounding London. In Surrey and other Home Counties, Conservatives were as hostile to L.C.C. expansion into their territory as the London Labour Party was suspicious. A rapidly formed Committee for London Government gathered well-known supporters to campaign against the enlargement of London, but despite their efforts, and vigorous filibustering in Parliament, the Conservative Government's London Government Act received the royal assent on 31 July 1963. Concessions had been made during the struggle: the average size of boroughs was increased from 150 000 to 250 000; the boundaries of Greater London were pulled tighter around the metropolis; the L.C.C.'s education functions were perpetuated by the newly created Inner

TABLE 6

The changing balance of political power in the London region

	Majority party in the pre-reform counties				
	1949	1952	1955	1958	1961
L.C.C.	Lab.	Lab.	Lab.	Lab.	Lab.
Middlesex C.C.	Con.	Con.	Con.	Lab.	Con.
Surrey C.C.	Con.	Con.	Con.	Con.	Con.
Kent C.C.	Con.	Con.	Con.	Con.	Con.
Essex C.C.	Ind.	Lab.	Con.	Lab.	Con.

	Majority party post-reform			
	1964	1967	1970	1973
G.L.C.	Lab.	Con.	Con.	Lab.

	Political majority in the 32 London boroughs (excluding the City of London)			
	1964	1968	1971	1974
Conservative	12	28	10	13
Labour	20	4	22	19

Source: F. Smallwood, *Greater London: the Politics of Metropolitan Reform*, 1965; *Annual Abstract of Greater London Statistics.*

London Education Authority (ILEA). Thereafter the newly named, amalgamated boroughs had to learn to live together: Labour Willesden was joined with Conservative Wembley to form Brent, Conservative Hornsey plus Labour Tottenham made Haringey, and so on. Contrary to Labour fears and Conservative expectations, the first Greater London Council was Labour-controlled.

Strategy and locality

Greater London has a two-tier government, with the Greater London Council (responsible for London as a whole) the top tier, and the London boroughs (responsible for local services) the lower tier. Part of the task of the Royal Commission, and subsequent parliamentary amendments to the slow-moving London Government Bill, was to define which tier was responsible for what. Broadly speaking, the G.L.C. became responsible for major highways, strategic planning, overspill housing, ambulance and fire services, sewers and drainage, and research and intelligence. Boroughs maintain local roads; supervise local planning; provide and manage local housing, personal social services, and libraries; levy and collect rates; and, in the case of twenty outer London boroughs, function as local education authorities.

A particular concern of this volume is to examine those aspects of metropolitan life which can be affected by land-use planning—the process of influencing the location of activities in *space* and their introduction, and removal, in *time*. Local government reorganization in Greater London brought a two-tier planning system which in 1974 was introduced throughout England and Wales. (Local government in Scotland was reorganized along different lines in 1975.) In the case of London, the G.L.C. was required to prepare a *Greater London Development Plan* (*G.L.D.P.*) into which total picture individual borough plans would lock, as in a jigsaw.

It so happens that the administrative and legal planning process in Britain is subject to scrutiny by the public at several stages in a way which other public sector services such as education, health, housing, social services, and transport, presently are not. Plans show the stages by which the present is to be transformed into a more desirable future. Now that the activities of central and local government and public corporations account for more than half of the country's national expenditure, and as most of the investment is transformed into buildings, roads, and services in the places where the people live, the future of urban areas is increasingly determined by public agencies. Thus any planning department has to canvas other central government and local authority departments—education, housing, and the rest—to find out about their future investment plans and land requirements. It needs emphasizing that planning departments approve, or reject, applications for change. Other council departments assemble and build on the land acquired either for comprehensive redevelopment or under the terms of the Community Land Act 1975.

The London Government Act 1963 required the G.L.C.'s Development Plan to 'lay down considerations of general policy with respect to the use of land in the various parts of Greater London, including in particular guidance as to the future road system'.

In August 1969 the G.L.C. presented the *G.L.D.P.* to the (then) Ministry of Housing and Local Government (now the Department of the Environment). The 'Plan' was actually a collection of documents:

1. *Written Statement*: an outline of the Council's policies.
2. *Report of Studies*: the supporting analysis of the problems of the metropolis, drawn from existing census and other published statistics and four of the G.L.C.'s own surveys into land use, housing, employment, and transport.
3. *Movement in London*: the methods and results of the London Transportation Study (the third phase of the London Traffic Survey which began in the early 1960s).
4. *Tomorrow's London*: an attractively written, illustrated essay on the tasks facing London government.
5. *Metropolitan Structure Map* (9 sheets), showing major land uses, action areas, areas of opportunity, and so on.
6. *Metropolitan Roads Map* (9 sheets), showing proposed motorways.
7. *High Buildings Map*, showing sensitivity to high buildings.

Even in 1969 the cost of the seven items was over £34, but copies were deposited at 104 libraries and borough offices throughout London for inspection. A period of three months until 9 December 1969 was allotted for the public to send objections to the Minister about some or all of the ingredients, and certain road objections were accepted until February 1970. Whereas the old L.C.C. Development Plan Inquiry of 1952 had provoked 6700 objections, the *G.L.D.P.* brought 28 392 objections from 19 997 objectors.

But the circumstances were different: three-quarters of the objections to the *G.L.D.P.* were directed at the road proposals, and a large proportion of these were from residents in south-east London whose housing or neighbourhood amenity was threatened by the proposed alignments.

The *G.L.D.P.*: assumptions and solutions

Population and employment. In the *Written Statement* the G.L.C. declared:

> It is the Council's intention to do everything within its power to maintain London's position as the capital of the nation and one of the world's great cities. It intends to foster the commercial and industrial prosperity of London and its cultural status, especially in respect of those functions for which a London location may be regarded as essential.

By 1969 certain clues were available to suggest that the society and economy of London was undergoing considerable change. The document showed that in Greater London, births exceeded deaths by 50 000 annually, but the natural increase was offset by a net loss through migration of 90 000 people a year (230 000 migrating to London each year; 320 000 emigrating)—a decline of 40 000 people a year over all. The loss was not just of people being displaced beyond the G.L.C. boundary as redevelopment brought lower densities in inner London: jobs were being lost as well. The *Written Statement* continued: 'If recent trends continue the population could be down to 7·0 million by 1981. This of itself might not be a cause for concern, but it would be accompanied by a reduction of about 700 000 in the resident labour force . . .' The Council hoped to be able to stem the flow and keep the figure at 7·3 million in 1981.* Fig. 12 shows the G.L.C.'s projection of population and employment published in 1969 with subsequent trends and more recent estimates. Table 5 in the previous chapter records how population estimates for 1981 published in 1975 were 800 000 below the 1969 *G.L.D.P.* figures. Recent employment estimates have likewise fallen beneath 1969 expectations. Alarmed by these seemingly uncontrollable centrifugal tendencies, the G.L.C. urged the removal of Office Development Permit controls and the relaxing of Industrial Development Certificate controls in London, seeking meanwhile the relocation of employment in outer London.

But the G.L.C. might derive some comfort from the knowledge that events often differ from projected trends. The decentralization of employment from central London to outer London and extra-London locations, combined with improved public transport services for commuters to the centre and reduced housing demand, could mean a less precipitous decline of population and employment than has been forecast recently. What the G.L.C. fears, understandably, is that fewer people will be left to produce the revenue for basic services like transport and education which have high running costs and extensive fixed capital and investment.

Housing. The G.L.C.'s 1967 housing survey for the *G.L.D.P.* identified the housing problem areas shown in Fig. 13. Census measures of overcrowding, multiple occupation of dwellings, and lack or sharing of basic facilities (bath, w.c., sink) were used to define areas of housing stress—which really implies social stress—and these, like the areas of housing in poor physical condition, are concentrated in inner London. Altogether 340 000 dwellings, 14 per cent of London's total housing stock, constitute the problem areas. Since 1969 there has been a shift in housing policy away from redevelopment (knocking down) towards rehabilitation, i.e. extending the life of the existing properties. In addition to seeking improvements within London, the Council intended to continue the planned yearly overspill of 20 000 people to New and Expanding Towns beyond the G.L.C. boundary.

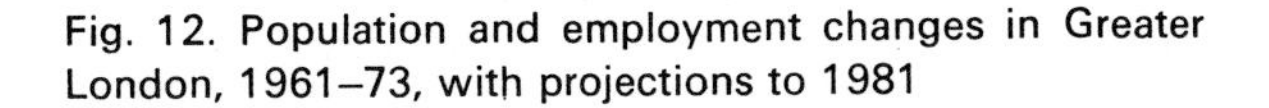

Fig. 12. Population and employment changes in Greater London, 1961–73, with projections to 1981

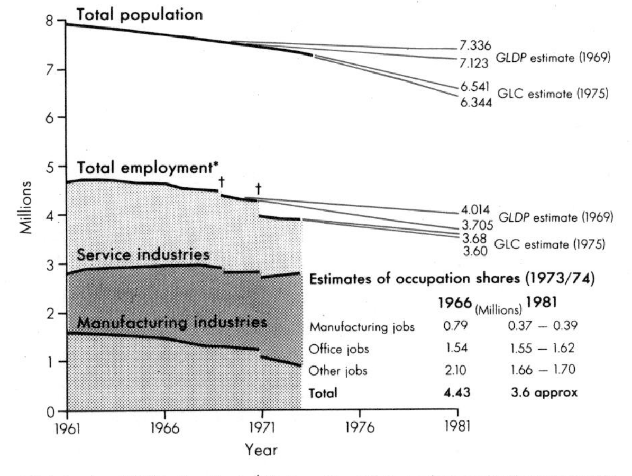

* Excludes about 250,000 self-employed † The base of the statistics has been modified from time to time

* In forecasting the population of Greater London the Council used novel estimates of the habitable rooms in the future housing stock as well as the traditional method of estimating the rates of household formation, births, deaths, and migration.

Not surprisingly, this policy is now thought to be counter-productive, especially by a growing number of councillors who express alarm at the rate of the decline of population and employment in Greater London.

Transport. The terms of reference of the *G.L.D.P.* required roads to be a dominant part of the strategy for London's future. After predicting that two-thirds of households in the London Transportation Study region would have use of at least one car by 1981 (compared with 42 per cent in 1966 and 54 per cent in 1971), and that in the period 1962–81 the total distance travelled by these vehicles would increase by 30 per cent in the central area and 160 per cent in the rest of the London Transportation Study area, road vehicles were to be given a greatly extended motorway system along which to move. (London's road inheritance is Roman, medieval, and Georgian; few purpose-built roads have appeared in the last century.) Ringway 1, the inner 'motorway box' fringing the central area; Ringway 2, the improved North and South Circular Roads about 12 km from the centre; and Ringway 3, about 20 km from the centre of London, were to be linked inwards to London and outwards to the rest of the country by a lattice of radial roads. This primary network of 500 km was estimated to cost about £1100 million (at 1970 prices), with another £500 million for an improved secondary network of about 1600 km. An estimated 50 000 people would be displaced by construction of the primary network. One comment on the ringways by the anonymous author of *Tomorrow's London* deserves close attention: '. . . the examination syllabus to which our secondary schools have to work still ensures that pupils can draw an intelligible map of the mouth of the Orinoco, but not of the London ringways system.'

The number of commuters travelling by British Rail (overground) and London Transport (underground) was likely to fall slightly as population decreased. Improvements to passenger interchanges were envisaged, but until 1970 when it took over control of London Transport, the Council exerted little direct influence on public transport.

Other problems were also considered by the G.L.C. in the *G.L.D.P.* documents, such as the desirability of developing major shopping and employment centres away from the centre, the location of wholesale markets, the conservation of buildings, the preservation and development of open spaces including the Green Belt, and the recreational use of waterways.

The *G.L.D.P.* inquiry: Layfield's views

Both the complexity of planning for London, and the number of objections, required the longest public inquiry into planning proposals ever held in Britain. From 7 July 1970 to 9 May 1972 a five-member inquiry panel and their chairman, Frank Layfield, Q.C., supported by five technical assessors, listened to witnesses at 326 appearances, discussed written objections, examined the Plan, visited all parts of London where motorways were proposed—and even visited Düsseldorf, Frankfurt, Hamburg, and Stockholm to see how city planners elsewhere were tackling tasks of restructuring. With commendable speed the panel delivered its report to the Secretary of State for the Environment in December 1972, who in turn made it public in February 1973.

Whilst recognizing that the *G.L.D.P.* was a prototype structure plan, and that the G.L.C. had been given hardly any guidance about its detailed contents, the Layfield panel were highly critical of the *Written Statement* and Maps. 'Grave defects' were exposed in the uncompromising *Report of the Panel of Inquiry*. Specifically, they believed that the *G.L.D.P.* had tried to do more than it could actually do. They stated that since it was unable to change established population trends, so it was unable to forecast employment supply and demand with any precision. (This is not to say that metropolitan planners should not try to influence households, firms, and governments by pointing to the unwelcome consequences of accelerated or uncontrolled decline.) There was a failure to relate information to policies. Technical information usually gives rise to a choice of policies, one of which may be preferred politically, but not so in the *G.L.D.P.* Policies were not related to aims, indeed the aims were not often clear, being framed in such general terms—'not to offend anyone too deeply'—that the panel declared the *Written Statement* 'can mean anything to anyone'.

Equally, though, criticisms can be directed at the inquiry, and the panel agreed that the cross-examination used made the debate about the future London more defensive than constructive: the G.L.C. became a petitioner. The G.L.C.'s *Written Statement* and *Report of Studies* were perforce based on 1961 and 1966 census data, yet in the late 1960s London's population and employment were waning quite dramatically. A revised *Written Statement* was issued by the G.L.C. in February 1972, and although its appearance was too late, the document went part

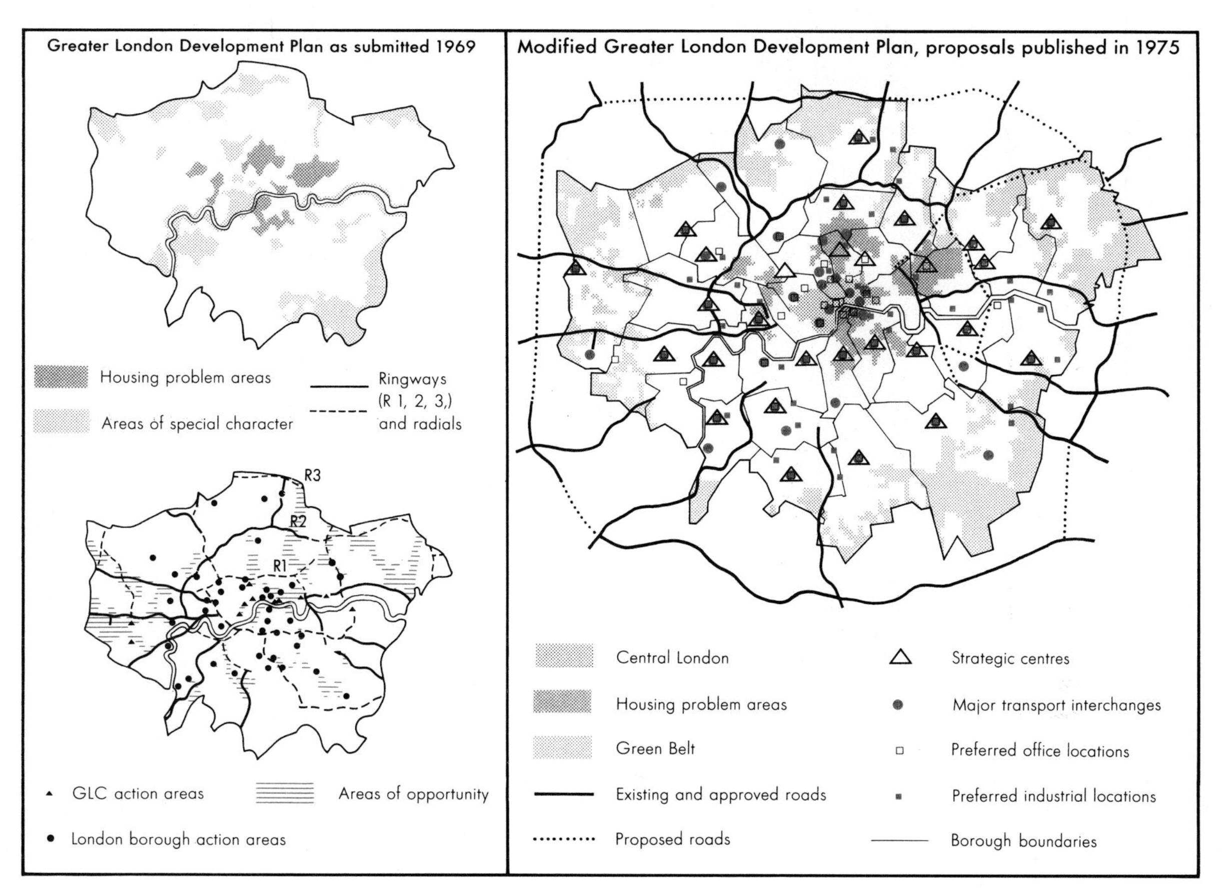

Fig. 13. Elements of Greater London's proposed physical structure, 1969 and 1975

way towards answering some of the Layfield dissatisfactions with the G.L.C.'s evidence and analysis.

The Layfield panel offered a rewritten Statement and new structure diagram to replace the Metropolitan Structure Map in their two-volume, 1375-page report. In their view the decline of London's population was not a cause for alarm, nor could they endorse the view of witnesses that middle-income and middle-aged groups were being squeezed out of London to leave behind a polarized population of rich and poor. But the migration tables of the 1971 census confirm London's centripetal attraction of the young and single and centrifugal displacement of the married and their families beyond the G.L.C. boundary. It becomes a matter of judgement to decide if the centrifuge is whirling too quickly. The panel also gave reasons why the G.L.C. could not hope to maintain levels of employment through floorspace controls, and urged the concerted rehabilitation of outworn industrial areas.

Two problems were basic to the continuing scourge of bad housing in London: the increasing rate of obsolescence in the housing stock and the disproportionate distribution of poor housing conditions in the privately rented sector. To overcome the first, an expanded rehabilitation programme was urged; for the second, the private sector must be supported. A new, powerful housing authority was proposed for London.

For transport the panel emphasized the desirability of an integrated strategy to link public transport policy, the management and restraint of traffic, environmental improvement, and road construction. As with housing, a new body for transport policy was thought desirable. Ringway 1 was supported, the upgrading of the North Circular Road agreed to, and north and south orbital roads around London supported in preference to Ringway 3.

Six 'major strategic centres' outside central London had been identified by the G.L.C. on the basis of their shopping turnovers: Ealing,

John Laing & Son Ltd.

Westway, here shown under construction in 1967, is one of the few completed sections of London's proposed Ringway 1 —the inner motorway box. Public opinion and local authority penury have brought motorway construction in inner London to a halt

Croydon, Ilford, Kingston, Lewisham, and Wood Green. Layfield endorsed the first four as being suitable locations for new commercial and industrial investment. A final and important recommendation was that the G.L.C. should establish an effective system of monitoring—a means of judging the success of particular policies.

Dismantling the *G.L.D.P.*

The G.L.C. was ten years old in April 1975, yet on that birthday there was still no detailed statement from the Department of the Environment on the acceptability or otherwise of the *G.L.D.P.*, despite the fact that boroughs were actively preparing borough plans. In February 1973 the Secretary of State for the Environment gave the Government's initial observations at the same time as he made the Layfield report public. But after that, first the G.L.C., and then the national government, was transferred from Conservative to Labour control. The new Labour-controlled G.L.C. questioned the assumptions behind the *G.L.D.P.*, as they had every right to do, for structure plans are not apolitical. They are about investment priorities which may advantage or disadvantage people depending on where they live and work.

The approval of the Department of the Environment is required for all structure plans, and the Secretary of State for the Environment's preferred revisions of the *G.L.D.P.* were published in December 1975 as the *Modified Greater London Development Plan* (*M.G.L.D.P.*), and included the Draft Key Diagram summarized in Fig. 13. The public was again given time in which to comment on the modifications—largely an amalgam of the G.L.C.'s 1972 revisions to the original *Written Statement* and the Layfield proposals—and it is anticipated that a document substantially the same as the *M.G.L.D.P.* will be adopted as the definitive Greater London Development Plan. In the absence of an approved structure plan, policies for London's roads, rail-

Greater London Council

Pedestrians and vehicles generally vie for space on the congested roads of central London. Parts of Oxford Street have been reserved for buses and taxis, and neighbouring South Molton Street has been pedestrianized for the improved convenience and safety of shoppers

ways, and housing have been revised in response to changing circumstances, as outlined in the remainder of this chapter. Indeed, the economic prosperity of parts of London seemed so faded in 1975 in comparison with the inquiry period (1970–2) that even a plan approved in, say, 1973 would have required amendment as 'monitoring' showed several of its assumptions to be rendered untenable.

Abandoning motorways

In February 1973 the Conservative Minister had accepted in outline the need for Ringway 1—his successors did not. In July 1973 the Labour G.L.C. announced the abandonment of 'reckless and irrelevant' motorway building in London in keeping with their pre-election manifesto. Little more than a year later, the Professional Institutions Council for Conservation was asking: what are the environmental consequences of *not* building motorways? Despite rises in the cost of fuel, car ownership and use are still increasing, and the design and engineering professions suggested that growing traffic might have as deleterious an effect on localities as motorways would have done. For its part, the G.L.C. realized that if there was to be no more additional road space built, then vehicle use would have to be restrained, especially in the congested central area at peak periods. Accordingly, a discussion paper on supplementary licensing was unveiled in 1975 which described a way of charging vehicles entering central London between 8 a.m. and 6 p.m. on Mondays to Fridays. London's politicians and transport planners are moving in the direction urged by J. Michael Thomson and others from the London Amenity and Transport Association in their book *Motorways in London* (1969). Being concerned primarily with people's dissatisfaction with public transport, LATA favoured a transport strategy directed at restricting cars and subsidizing fares in the centre, and improving roads in outer London. Wider support was shown in a survey by Peter Willmott and Michael Young in 1970. Only 9 per cent of a sample 1102 Londoners supported building new motorways inside London. By contrast, 65 per cent supported giving more help to old people as a priority, followed by 59 per cent who wanted to see more new homes built.

Railway co-ordination

Although the G.L.C. co-ordinates the finance and policy on London Transport's buses and underground, it has little direct influence on British Rail policy, although it can make grants to British Rail for passenger services. In the *London Rail Study* published in 1974, a study team chaired by Sir David Barran reported on investment options for London's railways towards the end of the century. This joint G.L.C./D.o.E./London Transport/British Rail study showed how the Thames railway watershed might be breached by a King's Cross–Waterloo link ('crossrail'), and how east–west links ('throughrail'), could further facilitate passenger interchange. Even if investment cannot be raised for these and the proposed River/Fleet and Chelsea/Hackney underground network extensions, the need to maintain staffing levels, to improve interchanges, and to modernize the system remains.

Towards a housing strategy

Similar problems of fragmented responsibility bedevil attempts to bring rapid improvements to London's housing problems. In 1965 the Sir Milner Holland Committee on Housing in Greater London underlined the fact that housing, slum clearance, landlord and tenant relationships, and planning for comprehensive redevelopment had all grown up under different statutes with no apparent co-ordination. The G.L.C.'s *Strategic Housing Plan* (December 1974) sought a continued house building and conversion programme, especially for low- and middle-income Londoners; extended public control of privately rented accommodation; a major effort to ensure that rehabilitation keeps pace with rates of obsolescence; improved mobility between the different types of tenure and the various parts of London; urgent help for the homeless; and better co-operation with the construction industry. The aims are tenable, but the flow of cash is presently impeded. Nevertheless, it is likely that, through conversion and new construction, there will be nearly a quarter of a million more dwellings in Greater London in 1981 (2 723 000 dwellings in total) than in 1971.

In theory this should ease the situation of London's homeless (11 900 homeless families applied for accommodation in 1972–3; just over half were housed by borough social services and housing departments), squatters (possibly 20 000 in 1974), and people in the bulk of the 120 000 dwellings that were officially 'unfit' at the time of the G.L.C.'s housing survey (1967). All too often, immigrants and their London-born families are trapped in bad, private housing. Vigilance will be needed to ensure that the sour American jibe that 'urban renewal means black removal' has no currency in London. There is evidence that even where immigrants are rehoused by public authorities, they are disproportionately clustered in old public housing.

One key to London's housing problems has been omitted from the narrative so far. According to the G.L.C.'s preparatory studies for the *G.L.D.P.*, the greatest opportunity for solving London's housing problems was in making land available in outer London boroughs for housing people displaced from inner London. The *Written Statement* took the force out of this recommendation, and offered an anodyne about the G.L.C. simply looking to the outer boroughs for assistance. Inner versus outer London conflicts have been built into the G.L.C. from its inception, as described at the beginning of this chapter.

From these various criticisms it is evident that the process of crystallizing a structure plan for Greater London is slow and difficult. If it were simply a matter of physical design and building to target dates, it would not be so arduous; but the task of 'fostering the commercial and industrial prosperity of the metropolis and its cultural status', although abetted by the planning machine, requires an amalgam of political will and individual initiative which can never be pre-ordained.

The prospects for renovating and enhancing the physical and social conditions of London are examined further in Chapter 6 following two case studies which illustrate the difficulties of deciding what is desirable redevelopment in terms of the balance between preservation and change, and between public and private investment.

5 Two Case Studies of Change

It should be readily apparent that just because a good planning idea or building project has been published, there is no guarantee that actual development will take the form first envisaged by the planning authority or the designers. Indeed, a recurring criticism of land-use planning as it has evolved in Britain is that it simply allows or resists development proposals instead of positively promoting a higher quality environment. As has been demonstrated in the case of the *Greater London Development Plan*, planning documents often overstate the planners' ability to regulate the operation of the land market.

Two case studies are now presented to demonstrate how recent appraisals of the redevelopment potential of contrasting areas of London have been modified quite fundamentally as a result of changes in the political balance of power, planning fashions, and the availability of finance.

Both areas are familiar to non-Londoners: Covent Garden is synonymous with the fruit and vegetable market which has now vacated WC2 for Nine Elms, and with the Opera House which remains; whilst the upstream docklands of east London, which begin at Tower Bridge, are illustrated in all elementary geographical texts about London but have now been overtaken by closures.

Covent Garden

Covent Garden was originally a convent garden belonging to the Abbey of Westminster. In spite of stringent, early-seventeenth-century building controls, the Earl of Bedford negotiated a licence to build houses on the edge of the expanding metropolis. Inigo Jones, Surveyor to the King, designed London's first town square around the elongated east–west 'piazza'. The wall of Bedford House garden closed the piazza to the south, arcaded town houses formed the east and north sides, and St. Paul's church formed the western frame of the ornamental whole.

A century later the area had lost its gentility: the third plate of Hogarth's *Rake's Progress* depicts a Covent Garden tavern. Most of the buildings in the Covent Garden area date from the nineteenth century. The old market was covered over in 1830; the 1858 Opera House is the third on that site (the other two having burnt down). In November 1974 the activities of traders and administrators in Covent Garden market moved to Nine Elms, Battersea.

Although the old market directly occupied only about 6 out of the 36 ha of the area, market activities gave Covent Garden much of its distinctive character. Lorry- and container-loads of fruit and vegetables would start arriving at about 11 p.m. and jostle for the limited parking space around the central market building. Porters off-loaded the provisions. Trading would be well under way by 5 a.m. as goods cascaded along the chain from grower and shipper to wholesale-supplier and retailer. So Covent Garden was not just a centre of night life—theatres and restaurants—but, like Fleet Street with its newspaper printing houses, a centre for night work in the heart of the metropolis. The New Covent Garden Market site at Nine Elms provides parking for 2000 lorries and 1000 cars. Fork-lift trucks are in common use: only on biscuit tins and tea-towels does one now see porters carrying baskets on their heads. The Nine Elms site is also bisected by railway tracks, although there has been delay in connecting the market to the railway network. With the waning of interest in a rail link to Europe via a Channel tunnel, the possibility of bringing peaches from Bologna by rail to London in ten hours has receded rapidly.

Knowing that the market intended to leave the cramped Covent Garden premises, the Greater London Council and the two local boroughs, Camden and the City of Westminster, formed a planning team to prepare a draft plan, which was published in 1968. The planning team had seven objectives for the area: to retain a lively mixed-use character; to increase residential accommodation substantially; to provide new public open space; to help ease traffic congestion in central London; to segregate—and also connect—pedestrians and vehicles; to integrate new development into the old-established activities which rely on the area's location and character; and, finally, to retain groups of buildings of architectural and historic importance.

To achieve this, the draft plan foresaw the rebuilding of 20 of the 36 ha of the Covent Garden area over a fifteen-year period. Private development would account for £103 million or nearly 80 per cent of the total cost, estimated at £141 million. The total floorspace would rise from

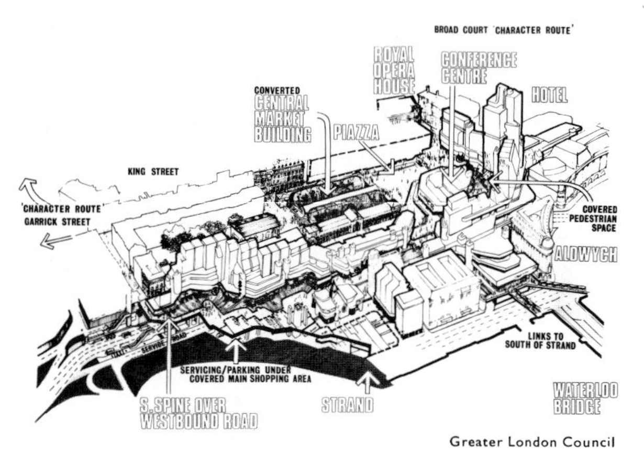

Greater London Council

Piecemeal change replaces the Covent Garden plan, 1968

1·16 million to 1·39 million m², and require an additional 140 000 m² of car-parking space. A new low-level, east-west road was proposed to relieve congestion in the Strand, and housing would be increased from 1300 to 3000 dwellings.

Between July and September 1971 a public local inquiry was held into the proposals of the revised plan—a slightly modified version of the 1968 draft. Local groups protested at the scale of the proposed change, and pleaded for less destruction. Then, while the decision of the Secretary of State for the Environment on the inquiry was awaited, Lady Dartmouth, the Chairman of the Covent Garden Joint Committee (a body representing the G.L.C., Camden, and Westminster, which was created in 1970 to co-ordinate the redevelopment activity) resigned. In her letter of resignation to the leader of the then Conservative-controlled G.L.C., she wrote: '. . . No individuals or bodies who represent the general public have supported us, and I have felt increasingly that our proposals are out of date and out of tune with public opinion.' As an alternative, she and some of her Joint Committee colleagues suggested that the G.L.C. should have powers over only the 6 ha then belonging to the Covent Garden Market Authority which the G.L.C. had agreed to buy when the market was relocated.

Conservation ousts redevelopment

The Secretary of State for the Environment reported in January 1973. He agreed that Covent Garden should be designated formally as a 'Comprehensive Development Area' (within which the local authority can make an order for the compulsory acquisition of land), but considered that more emphasis should be given to conservation. Later that month about 250 buildings were added to the list of buildings of special architectural or historic interest, adding weight to the Minister's purpose. The Minister doubted the need to expand shopping space from 78 400 to 129 000 m², whilst the proposals for hotels (to be increased from 4900 to 134 000 m²) and main roads seemed overambitious. So the redevelopment proposals were sent back to the drawing-board for the incorporation of the buildings newly listed for preservation (Fig. 14). The local residents' and workers' viewpoints will have much more force in the new plans.

Following the recommendations of the Skeffington Committee on Public Participation in Planning (1969), a Covent Garden Forum was elected in June 1974, whose representatives are a sounding board for resident tenants, owners and leaseholders, employees, and managers in business and services. People living and working in the area are eligible to register as electors for the Forum, and many of those elected have 'battled' already against the draft proposals as members of the Covent Garden Community Association. There are to be six technical stages in replanning Covent Garden—survey, defining objectives, presenting a range of options, selecting a preferred draft plan, developing it into a local plan and holding an inquiry, and implementation—and at each stage the views of the Forum will be solicited.

But why is a Forum needed? Surely local councillors are elected to receive and deal with local wishes and grievances? It has to be remembered, however, that in a metropolis such as London, borough councillors may represent 4000 people, and the two or three Greater London councillors elected from each borough using parliamentary constituency boundaries, represent on average 80 000 people. So the interests of people in an area as small as Covent Garden need a purpose-built local body through which to voice their aspirations for the area's physical fabric and social life. Both within Covent Garden and outside it there has been pressure since the late 1960s for the creation of neighbourhood councils in urban areas, broadly analogous to parish councils in rural areas. (The financial powers of parish councils are few and modest; their primary role is that of commenting on proposals for change in their locality.)

Since December 1974 the Forum has had its own administrative secretary, office, and newspaper in Covent Garden, all provided at the G.L.C.'s expense. Interestingly, the planning team for Covent Garden has operated from offices in the area since the G.L.C./Camden/West-

Greater London Council

Covent Garden without the market has resembled a seaside resort out of season, but the central market buildings are **being** renovated to provide small specialist shops

minster study was inaugurated in 1965. Nowadays, planners and politicians are increasingly aware of the importance of G. K. Chesterton's dictum that 'to make something real, you have to make it local'. There is ample evidence that more planning will be done by teams in local offices where the professional civic designers are better placed to sense local feeling. In passing, it is interesting to note how the more radical pressure groups—which often label themselves 'action' groups—are more often than not campaigning for inaction: to save the present small-scale and jumbled activities against future action which implies the threat of gigantism and uniformity. In the case of Covent Garden, the Community Association's spirited offensive against wholesale demolition continued long enough for the Secretary of State for the Environment to echo public opinion at large in the move towards conservation and piecemeal redevelopment and away from the grandiose restructuring of the metropolitan fabric. And the downswing in the property market and public spending in the mid-1970s offered financial reinforcement to the new aesthetic mood.

Fig. 14. Covent Garden conservation proposals, 1973

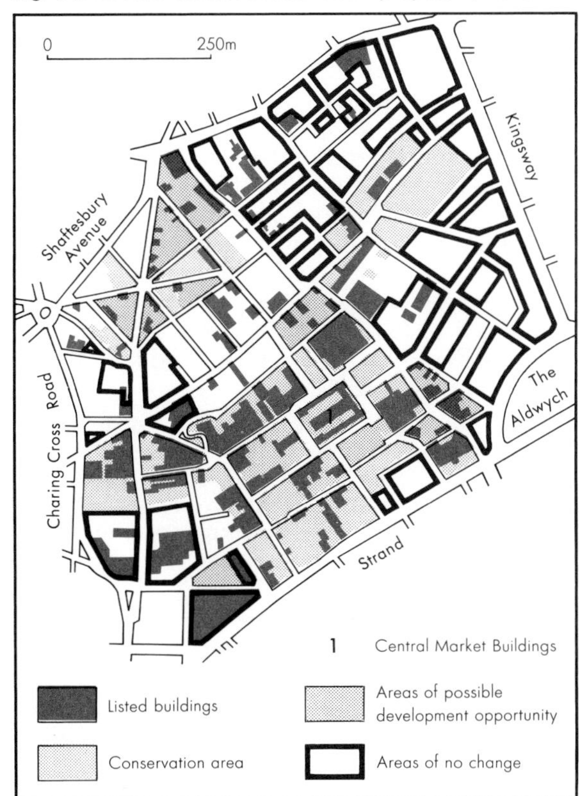

Even if the face of Covent Garden is to change less dramatically than was proposed in 1968, the urgency of improving the existing housing remains. A G.L.C. survey of most of the 1400 households (a 'household' shares a common housekeeping budget) showed that 12 per cent did not have their own cold water, 28 per cent lacked their own hot water, and 20 per cent had to share a toilet with another household. One-fifth of 'heads of households' (meaning the principal wage-earner) worked unsocial hours, which implies that they help to run the public services and entertainments of London.

The case of Covent Garden shows that people with justifiably rising expectations do not have to be rehoused in ever-rising blocks of flats, even in the centre of the metropolis.

Ships can be seen berthed in the West India and Millwall, and in the Royal docks, but the London and the Surrey Comme

Docklands

The Covent Garden study area totals less than 50 ha. Recent planning history there shows how difficult it is to restructure such a densely built-over part of central London. About 5 km east of Covent Garden lie the docklands, adjacent to the River Thames in east London. Disused docks and vacant land surplus to the requirements of gas and electricity boards total about 1300 ha in a 2200 ha dockland area between Tower Bridge and Barking Creek. If restructuring Covent Garden is such a protracted and difficult operation, what chance is there of redeveloping 1300 ha in an 11-km long sector of the metropolis littered with massive dock installations?

London's earliest docks were on the north bank of the Thames within the City itself, but pilfering and the risk of fire in the wooden ships moored alongside the City wharves, led to demands for secure enclosed docks. Empty land was available downstream. So the docks were excavated in the marshy wastes of east London. Only St. Katharine's Dock, adjacent to the Tower of London, required large-scale destruction: 1200 dwellings housing over 11000 people were demolished for the docks and warehouses. It is some of these early-nineteenth-century docks that have closed (East India Dock 1967, London Docks and St. Katharine's Dock 1968, Surrey Commercial Docks 1970). The reasons are not difficult to see: the docks are cramped, the entrance locks narrow, and approach roads congested. In addition, the advent of containerization of seaborne cargo has favoured purpose-built container berths as at Tilbury. The future of even the docks on the Isle of Dogs and the extensive Royal group is uncertain.

Realizing that the dock closures in east London offered an opportunity to re-sort the jumble of industrial, transport, and residential land uses of the riverside area, the Secretary of State announced in Parliament in April 1971 that the Department of the Environment and the G.L.C. would jointly commission an

> urgent and comprehensive study of the potentialities for redevelopment of the whole of the riverside area—from London and Surrey Docks in the west, to Beckton in the east . . . The broad aim will be to achieve a balanced development and, above all, to improve for those living in the area, the quality of their environment.

Some 80 per cent of the Docklands Study Area, as defined for the comprehensive study, is owned by six public or semi-public authorities (Fig. 15). By far the most important is the Port of London Authority (P.L.A.) which, since 1909, has given unified control to the formerly private dock groups. The task of identifying the broad struc-

Aerofilms

ks lie idle awaiting redevelopment

tural elements of the future docklands—which might have no working docks within their bounds—fell to the consultancy firm of R. Travers Morgan and Partners whose report on the docklands was published in 1973. They emphasized that their principal concern was with community problems that could be solved by a plan which regulates the location, variety, and intensity of land uses. Their analysis, therefore, did not cover the broad aspects of health, education, and welfare policy which, as they rightly stated, are also of great importance in influencing the quality of life.

Problems and choices

The Travers Morgan team assumed that the India and Millwall Docks would be ripe for closure by 1977, the western Royal group likewise deserted by 1982, and dock closures in Beckton and North Woolwich completed by 1991. Thus nearly 1200 ha of P.L.A. and adjacent land would be available for redevelopment by 1991. What should the map of the docklands in 1991 look like? The answer is partly related to the problems of the immediate locality and inner London, problems which a fairly sudden release of land could be expected to ameliorate.

First-order problems identified by the team were principally housing shortage, the narrow choice of housing type and jobs, and the rather squalid living environment in the isolated dockland communities. (To use the word 'community' implies some level of social or physical cohesion: in the docklands this is achieved by the poor external transport connections of the riverside, if by nothing else.) Second-order problems include demands for transport, local shopping and leisure facilities, schools, and public services. Third-order problems include the technical and administrative problems of restructuring 1200 ha or more over a fourteen-year period (1978–91). Certainly, finding the public and private resources for the rebuilding, and assembling a design team of some 2500 people, are even more formidable problems than demolishing the hundred or so different types of massive dock wall or filling in 15–19 million of the 23 million m³ of actual dock.

Initially the team postulated eighteen possible ways of redesigning the map of the docklands of 1991. Each design could be evaluated according to how successfully it remedied the existing problems of the docklands area. Eventually the list was reduced to five options which reflected the broad choice of possible solutions. Fig. 15 shows how one of these possible plans for 1991, called 'Europa', would change the structure of the area. Being one of the most expensive

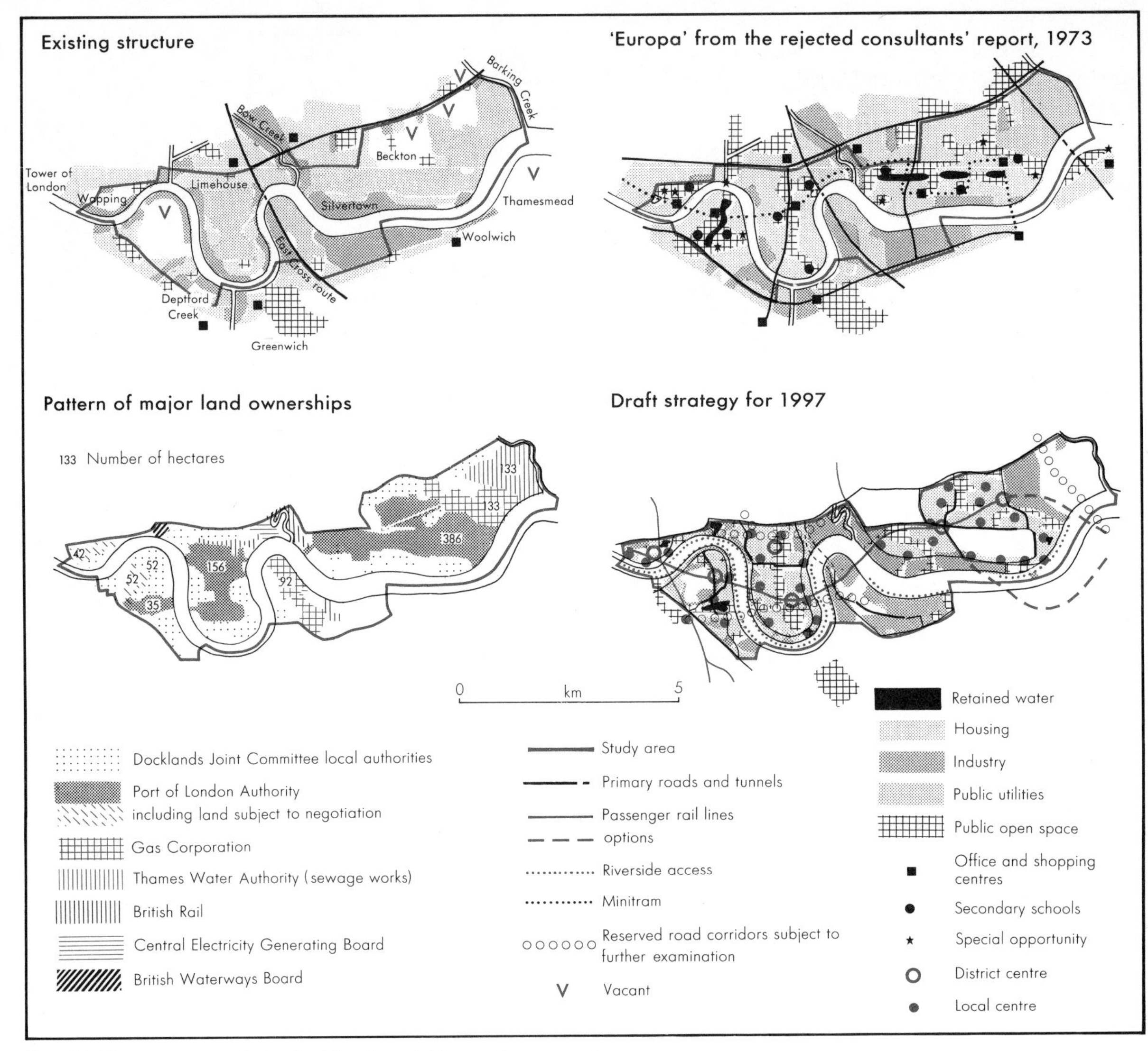

Fig. 15. The structure of the docklands: existing and proposed

schemes (£894 million at 1971 prices), and two-thirds of the new housing being in the private sector (the reverse of present tenure patterns in the docklands), it is perhaps a recipe for the ideal rather than the practicable. Certainly, such ingredients as parks and chains of lakes, and new service-sector jobs focused around stations on a minitram line would, in the team's words, 'greatly distinguish the area from the rest of east London'.

Whilst Travers Morgan were examining the possible choices for rebuilding the docklands, other influences were apparent in the eastern sector of the metropolis. The most important of these was the Government's choice in April 1971 of Foulness Island/Maplin Sands as the site for a new third London airport. This decision reversed earlier policy. Stansted had been chosen in May 1967, then rejected in May 1968, when the Government announced the creation of a Commission on the Third London Airport chaired by the Hon. Mr. Justice Roskill. The Commission had three questions to answer: Is a third airport needed? If so, by when, and where should it be located? It answered: Yes; 1980–2; and Cublington, respectively. Only one of the Commission members dissented: Professor Colin Buchanan preferred Foulness on the grounds that it might help to reduce the disparity between the east side of London and the much more favoured western side.

In July 1973 the Department of the Environment presented two public consultation documents on the Maplin project (as the Foulness airport was now called). One considered the possible area for a new city to serve the airport. It was estimated that the population of the Southend peninsula might increase from 300 000 to 600 000 over the period 1981–2001 as airport-generated employment also brought about rapid immigration. Such a level of growth was in accord with the *S.P.S.E.*'s major growth centre in south-east Essex, proposed to accommodate one million people at the end of the century. The second document examined possible alignments for transport access corridors from London to Maplin. King's Cross was the preferred site for the London high-speed rail link terminal, although an airport motorway could reach London from the north-east or along the Thames. Taken together, the dockland proposals and Maplin project would divert much of the resources of the construction industry in the South East region to the eastern sector of London over the next quarter century.

But in July 1974 the Maplin airport scheme was cancelled, though the Port of London Authority still expressed interest in building a seaport on the reclaimed sands. The Government explained that air traffic was not growing as quickly as had been anticipated, and that planes were carrying more passengers, so that fewer flights were needed. Stansted, reprieved from expansion seven years earlier, was again the favoured airport to supplement Heathrow and Gatwick, although this time there were no proposals to extend the length or number of runways.

So the collapse of population assumptions in the South East noted in Chapter 3 and with them the viability of the south-east Essex major growth centre, coupled with the abandonment of the Maplin project, means that the outer reaches of the Thamesside sector are unlikely to grow so rapidly. The docklands renewal scheme thereby becomes a London-scale problem rather than being the London end of a wider growth corridor. Fig. 16 shows the overlap of the several studies of the early 1970s, and identifies yet another study area. Tower Bridge to Tilbury came under the scrutiny of a Thamesside Conference (created in 1970) which issued a report in 1974 on ways of restructuring the 25 km of the riverside downstream from the Docklands Study Area. One applauds the coming together of local authority planners and politicians from the north and south banks of the lower Thames, but again assumptions about major growth in south-east Essex and medium growth in the Medway towns area are seen to be untenable. With less public and private investment available, the chances of encouraging 'co-ordinated development' and 'the use of land to best advantage' is severely limited.

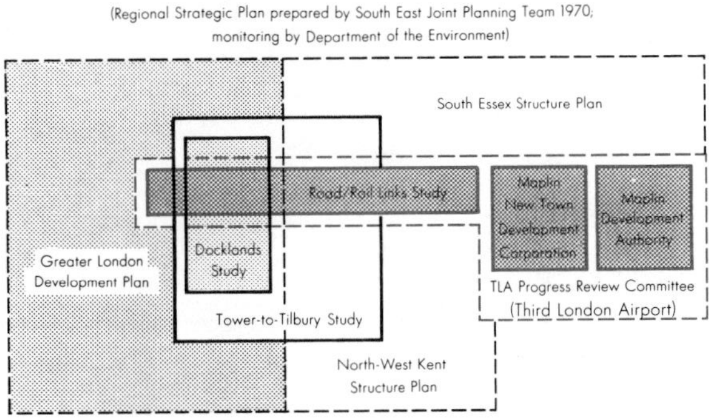

Fig. 16. Overlapping study areas in east London in the early 1970s

Towards a new strategy

Not only has the growth potential of the whole eastern sector of London been dimmed since 1974, but progress towards agreeing a strategy for the docklands has been slow. The new Labour G.L.C. of May 1973 saw the consultants' report as an initial analysis rather than a plan, and after a period of public consultation in the summer of 1973, the five options were discarded. A tripartite Docklands Joint Committee, comprising councillors from the G.L.C. and five dockland boroughs, together with nominees of the Secretary of State for the Environment, is now the political authority for dockland redevelopment. It is served by planners in a specially formed docklands development team. Just as the six Covent Garden local plan discussion papers and reports of survey were published for comment in 1974, so eight docklands working papers appeared in 1975 as part of the process of public consultation. It is anticipated that by the end of 1976 an agreed strategy for the development of the docklands will have been approved.

Ingredients

Already St. Katharine's Dock has been redeveloped, proposals for a World Trade Mart at Surrey Commercial Docks have been accepted, and Riverside London Ltd. has applied for planning permission for its scheme for London Docks. St. Katharine's Dock was sold by the Port of London Authority to the G.L.C. in 1969 for £1·7 million. The G.L.C. announced a competition for redevelopment schemes for

London World Trade Centre Association

An 826-bedroomed hotel, world trade centre, service apartments, timber-framed brewery restored as a restaurant, and a yacht haven for the partially completed St. Katharine-by-the-Tower redevelopment

the 10-ha site of largely intact dock walls and warehouses, and the Taylor Woodrow Property Company proposals were adjudged the most appropriate. Taylor Woodrow converted the P.L.A.'s St. Katharine Dock House into the World Trade Centre. The Ivory Warehouse has been restored as apartments: World Trade Centre members will be able to offer hospitality here to overseas clients. Across the dock, now a yachting marina, the riverfront adjacent to Tower Bridge is dominated by the 826-room Tower Hotel, an easterly outlier of the hotel boom described in Chapter 2. It is now thought that the St. Katharine's redevelopment should be complete by 1985, and it is expected to include 300 private and 400 local authority dwellings, a primary school, shops, and restaurants. Local pressure groups have protested that the starting of council house building (which will in any case be paid for by the G.L.C.) has been delayed in favour of the hotel and World Trade Centre.

Similar doubts about development costs, profit, and social benefit are expressed throughout the docklands area. Already the Surrey Commercial Docks and London Docks have been seen as valuable sites by prospective developers who envisage warehousing and distributive trades in addition to a similar mixture of offices, hotels, and public and private housing. The danger is that the three empty upstream or 'near east' docks—those close to the City—will be redeveloped quickly and profitably, largely by private finance, leaving the 'far east' wastes of north Greenwich, Woolwich, and Beckton for the local authorities to develop. The local authorities see in the vacant docklands a chance to shorten their housing lists, the registers of people in overcrowded, unhealthy, or unfit housing who want a council property. But the same local authorities are also anxious to see their rate income increased. Crudely stated, the more they collect, the more they have to finance house building and social services, and an office block does top up the rates.

Parliament's questions . . .

The Expenditure Committee of the House of Commons carefully scrutinizes spending by central and local government. In the spring of 1975 its Environment sub-committee invited evidence on three aspects of dockland redevelopment which are germane to any redevelopment effort in London: the level of financial support from central government that complete redevelopment would require, the type of agency that could best supervise the redevelopment, and the implications of dockland renewal for regional policy.

The consultants' report of 1973 had suggested public sector spending of £260–490 million (at 1971 price levels) for the five options. Between a quarter and a half of the public sector total would be spent on housing, and the rest on roads and transport, schools, and all other public services. Parliament was interested to know if such a level of spending, most of which is paid for by central government grants, could provide greater benefits for more people if spent outside the docklands, or outside London. Related to this are the regional development repercussions of the docklands. Is a local unemployment rate of 6–12 per cent (Great Britain 4·9; Poplar 12·0) recorded in employment exchanges in the dockland boroughs in October 1975 sufficiently high to justify the attraction of new industrial and commercial jobs to the docklands when government policy has been to steer as much industrial (and recently commercial) investment as possible away from Greater London? Hitherto the national view of Greater London has been of a single labour market with unemployment always significantly lower than the national average. To single out the docklands as an area for new jobs would require government acknowledgement that the industrial structure of the docklands is as unbalanced and antiquated as that in parts of the development areas. Would politicians in the latter areas agree?

Who should supervise the rebuilding of dockland? The responsibility was given to the Docklands Joint Committee in 1974, although some commentators advocated the creation of a special docklands agency with powers similar to a New Town development corporation. Development corporations are empowered to acquire land compulsorily at its existing use value (usually farmland, for conversion to residential and employment uses) rather than its market value (which for farmland with planning permission for housing can be as much as ten times its agricultural value). So land bought as empty warehouses and wet enclosures would be much cheaper than dockland bought with an eye to development. But critics of New Town development corporations say that their economic and administrative efficiency is achieved only by authoritarian control. If the message of public protest in the docklands can be simplified, it would probably read: 'Look first to the people who live and work here already. Safeguard their jobs; improve their homes . . .' Of course there is no reason why a dockland development corporation should not be responsive to local pressures; institutions, like businesses, have to adapt in order to survive.

. . . and Parliament's answers

The parliamentary sub-committee sifted evidence from the many statutory and spontaneous dockland bodies. They proposed that for the time being at least, the Docklands Joint Committee should continue to function, with augmented powers to acquire and dispose of land under the Community Land Act. The inquisitorial M.P.s did not think that the docklands deserved special status in national industrial location terms, but they did stress the importance of large-scale industrial retraining.

By early 1975 the estimated cost of renewing the docklands and doubling its population from 55 000 had risen to £1250 million over a fifteen-year period. (The draft docklands strategy of April 1976 raised the estimate to £2000 million by 1997.) With at least half the investment likely to be derived from public funds, the M.P.s' Environment sub-committee recommended that the Department of the Environment should give guidance at an early stage on the likely range and phasing of public expenditure. Another of their conclusions was that at a national level, insufficient interest is shown in the division of resources in a given region as between inner city redevelopment, town expansion, New Towns, and other major projects. Maybe this presages firmer guidelines from central government to regional planning councils on the 'best buy' priorities in regional public expenditure. With hindsight there is no doubt that London and the South East was incapable of finding money for the docklands, Maplin, ringways, and a Channel tunnel during the 1970s, even if the national economy had been buoyant rather than sluggish or besieged. And in conditions of sluggishness, which of these four projects individually, or which parts in combination, would have made the best use of scarce resources? Hitherto there has been no regional body to ask the question or attempt an answer by cost-benefit or any other welfare-accounting technique, or to assess environmental impact, although the Roskill Commission employed a variety of techniques on the single issue of the third London airport.

6 London's Future

One of the basic facts of metropolitan life is that although population turnover may be marked—there is a 30 per cent change annually in the electoral roll of the Earl's Court district of bed-sitters and flats—the physical form of London as a whole changes quite slowly. Perhaps only 1 per cent of the metropolis is rebuilt in any given year. But the rate of obsolescence will accelerate in future. Late-nineteenth-century London is being demolished or rehabilitated now, and this is already accompanied by the refurbishing of vast tracts of inter-war terraces in the suburbs. Grandiose plans are unlikely to be realized. Now that London's outward growth is curbed, the metropolis seems set for a future of piecemeal restructuring and reconstruction. Energy will increasingly be directed at the internal frontier of problem areas within the metropolis, but will also be coloured by considerations internal and external to the region identified in this chapter.

Looking to the future

Despite the current vogue for prediction, few books (as opposed to planning reports) have considered London's future, in contrast with the number that survey its past. Titles such as *The Future of London* (E. Carter, 1962), *London 2000*, and *Tomorrow's London* did appear in the 1960s, but the concern in the early 1970s has been more specific: *The Future of London's Past* or *The Future of London as an International Financial Centre* (Cabinet Office, 1973). Taken together, such writings consider broad social and political futures in a way which is often neglected by action-orientated planning reports. Britain as a whole, it might be noticed, has not shared in the outpouring of books on aspects of the present or impending 'urban crisis'—congestion, crime, overcrowding, pollution, poverty, racial tension—which has emanated from the United States since the mid-1960s.

British planners have not been as prolific as North American planners in experimenting with computer simulations of urban change which require rigorous study of the relationships between population and employment changes and transport demand. But alternative futures are being considered by generating hypothetical word-pictures or 'scenarios' of London future. The Central London Planning Conference, comprising boroughs within the statistical central area and the G.L.C., has been considering the far-reaching consequences of further office growth, more tourism, traffic restraint, and so on. Currently the problems of the continuing inner-city decline are more deserving of high priority on its agenda. If the public view on the future is sought, it is often easier for people to say what is undesirable than what is desirable. Congestion, blight, and overcrowding are tangible; the 'city beautiful' is not. Should London planning be driven more by the protester's abhorrence of the intolerable than by the aesthete's view of the ideal?

Planning and administration

In some ways London planning is moving in this direction. Master plans like the *G.L.D.P.* are adjudged out of favour in any case by fashionable planners. Plans for housing action areas and priority areas for education, immigration, and even recreation, are now preferred to broad strategic plans. Selective urban aid from the Home Office, Department of Education and Science, and Department of the Environment is directed into small areas. Lessons about co-ordinating local authority activities from the 'urban guidelines studies', carried out in Oldham, Rotherham, and Sunderland, are being heeded by London's planners and administrators. They are also following the investigation into powers, resources, and techniques in the continuing 'Inner Area Studies' of Lambeth, Birmingham, and Liverpool, and the 'Leisure Experiments' in four other selected centres. All these studies are concerned with getting better value for public expenditure and making sure that local government programmes help the people for whom they were designed.

In a real sense the G.L.C. should be the single strategic authority for London which can monitor changes and at least complain, if not intervene, should different boroughs' sectoral policies (planning, housing, education and welfare, and so on) either negate each other or accidentally conspire to leave particular areas or social groups within London unfairly disadvantaged. But in many ways the boroughs are increasingly autonomous. Critics have recently suggested that a 'Minister for London', appointed in Parliament, would be the only suitable umpire for adjudicating in actions disputed by the G.L.C. and boroughs. In France the President of the Republic exerts such powers over Paris.

Although the G.L.C.'s powers are defined more by consent than statute, its boundaries are firmly fixed, and while most commentators agree that the G.L.C. is too small, they also agree that further boundary revision is presently out of the question. Derek Senior advocated a metropolitan planning area intermediate in size between the G.L.C. and South East region, stretching from Newbury to Maplin and from Royston to the South Downs, in his weighty volume of dissent to the Royal Commission on Local Government in England, 1966–9, but his well-designed hull was never launched. So the G.L.C. remained a strategic planning authority without an agreed planning strategy even on its tenth birthday. Admittedly it has published discussion papers in the series 'London: The Future and You', in addition to Green Papers on topics like road pricing, lorry routes, and public transport fares. But the G.L.C. spends little money mounting exhibitions concerned with London's future (cf. Amsterdam), or publishing a regular magazine about recent and projected developments (cf. the Ruhr Planning Authority), or even encouraging a short list of schemes for 'London in the year 2000' to appear in tourist brochures (cf. Paris).

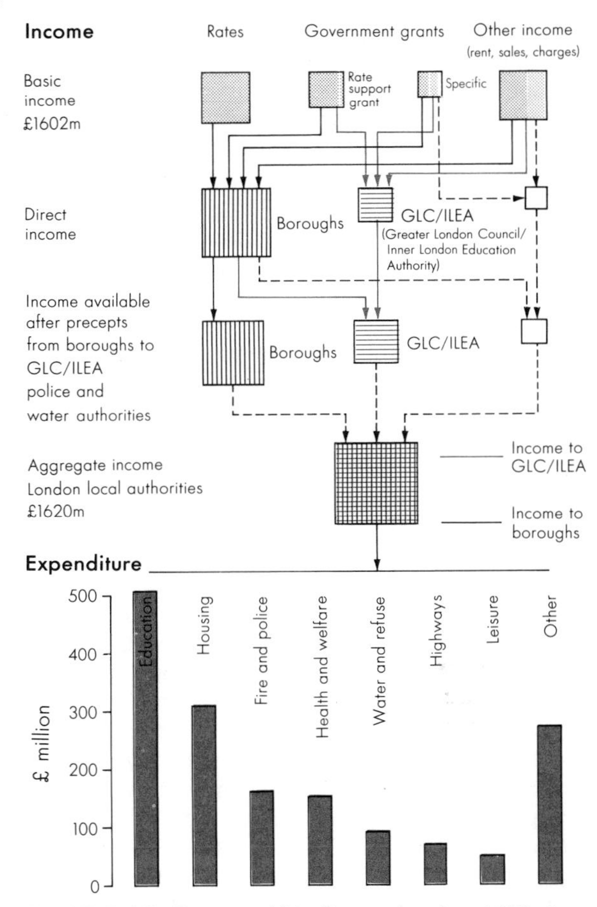

Fig. 17. Public finance within Greater London, 1972–3

Finance and politics

Politics, said Napoleon, is the difficult art of making things work. It is not just the art of the possible; but the art of achievement, which needs resources of energy and money. The latter is in short supply in London and just before the 1975 E.E.C. referendum, the G.L.C. was borrowing money in the Eurobond market to pay for its many activities (Fig. 17).

Boroughs levy and collect rates on property of all kinds, and this is supplemented by government grants and miscellaneous receipts. The rateable value of London boroughs in 1974–5 ranged from £312 million (Westminster) to £26 million (Sutton). It has to be remembered that central boroughs provide numerous services for their excess daytime population, but the whole rating system has been reviewed during 1974–5 by the Layfield Committee to see how a fairer match can be achieved between a local authority's needs and its financial resources.

The balance of existing rate burdens within London once again shows discrepancies between a rich West End, a poor East End and inner South, and the more affluent outer suburbs. As people and jobs leave inner London, so does their money. Increasingly the elderly, poor, and unskilled are left in inner areas, exacerbating the strains on impoverished boroughs and underused transport systems. A social mix may be political anathema to some London boroughs, but where it is achieved it means that individual householders help to pay for renovating small patches within the metropolis without excessive demands on the local authority.

The short-term future is more firmly fixed than politicians may like to admit. A party in opposition can proclaim the benefits of uniform cheap fares on public transport: when in power and trying to balance the books it is less easy. Some 70 per cent of the £1325 million G.L.C. budget in 1974–5 (excluding the running of the Inner London Education Authority and the London Transport Executive) was 'revenue expenditure', that is money spent running the public services. Even within the remaining 30 per cent of 'capital expenditure', which relies on borrowed capital, it is difficult to rapidly reorder the priorities between housing, school building, roads, and public transport. In times of stringency, however, it is inevitably housing and education services that face cuts rather than the essential welfare, police, fire, and water services.

Prices and employment

It is reasonable to assume that London's population is continuing to fall, both as a result of planned movements to New and Expanding Towns and by continuing voluntary emigration, triggered by a combination of dissatisfaction with the cost and strains of metropolitan living or the positive lure of pay or housing conditions elsewhere. Mindful of the critical labour shortages in the public sector in recent years (especially police, Post Office, teaching, and transport—British Rail and London Transport underground were short of 21 per cent and 12 per cent of guards, respectively, in autumn 1974), the Pay Board's Advisory Report, *London Weighting*, in 1974 recommended that public employees working within 6·4 km of Charing Cross receive a London weighting of £400, with £200 for those in outer London. This special addition to their income would lead to comparability of real earnings between London and elsewhere, it being shown that public sector workers in inner London paid an average of £431 a year for housing compared with £290 in the rest of the country, and £153 a year for an average 50-minute journey to work of 17·7 km. Outside London the average is £80 for a journey of 27 minutes and 8·5 km. To the £141 and £73 housing and travel differentials was added £81 for other items of consumer expenditure and £105 for wear and tear in travelling to work and compensation for lower standards of housing.

Although the weighting has helped the public employee's household budget, it has been of little help to newly married couples and others wanting to buy a first house. Basic London house prices are still often double those asked elsewhere for properties of similar size, age, and amenity, mainly because of inflated land costs in London, and so double the deposit is required. Relatively lower house prices in the Outer Metropolitan Area have made many purchasers trade off the reduced deposit and mortgage required against the higher travel costs on a journey to central London. Statistical confirmation of this is given by the migration tables of the 1971 census: 58 per cent of out-migrants from the G.L.C. to the O.M.A., 1966–71, were in the two age-bands 20–34 (mainly young parents) and 5–14 (their young children).

Whether or not the London weighting adds to inflation, many public and private employers will continue to give allowances or subsidized accommodation in order to recruit and hold employees in London. Such actions—and indeed the whole weighting exercise—may never be related to the *G.L.D.P.*

Hinterland and foreland

The concept of hinterland and foreland derives from port studies. In addition to being a port, London is also an entrepôt for ideas and market intelligence which enables the City to specialize in exchanging invisible titles to goods and property rather than the goods themselves. London's future dominance as a centre of finance and government is often discussed; here we concentrate on government. Decisions from Whitehall and Parliament filter down the command hierarchies of local government in Britain. Should London always dominate? Successive governments have thought not, and have sought to disperse and decentralize government functions to the provinces. Dispersal involves moving work—whole departments such as the Post Office Savings Bank, Civil Service Commission, or Ordnance Survey. Decentralization is less about saving money on high London rents, and more about devolving decision-making to the regions in the way approved by Lord Kilbrandon's Royal Commission on the Constitution (1973). After analysing personal and telephone contact patterns, transport connections with London, and qualitative factors such as job opportunities for women in London compared with elsewhere, Sir Henry Hardman reported in 1973 that 30 000 out of 86 000 civil service jobs in London departments could be moved from London. Negotiations continue, with some civil servants concerned about promotion prospects outside London.

Looking at relocation from the provincial regions' point of view, John Goddard (1975) has shown that concentrated decentralization is desirable. Four-fifths of journeys for business meetings in central London take less than 30 minutes; numerous supporting clerical, data-processing, and publicity services are at hand. Unless so-called 'contact environments' and services are built up in regional centres, London will continue to dominate nationally in the quaternary (decision-making) sector of economic activity. But unlike government agencies, private firms decentralizing from (mainly) inner London locations, whether to expand or to save rent, have so far stayed close to London. Of the 1615 relocating firms which consulted the Location of Offices Bureau in the period 1963–74, 42 per cent removed to another Greater London address, 33 per cent to the Outer Metropolitan Area, and only 10 per cent to destinations in the other ten regions of the United Kingdom (although these regions have attracted 24 per cent of the 133 248 jobs involved).

Turning away from London's national hinterland to its international foreland, the metropolis is obviously the focus in the United Kingdom for diplomatic and trade contacts and for international communications of all kinds. It competes for the headquarters of European organizations with the other European capitals, and in spite of Anglophone business language advantages, concedes institutions of Francophone diplomacy to Geneva (EFTA, GATT, W.H.O., and United Nations Economic Commission for Europe), Paris (UNESCO, O.E.C.D., I.M.F., and World Bank Europe), and Brussels (NATO and Commission of the European Communities). At the height of the office boom in the early 1970s, prestige office rents in London averaged £86 per m^2 per year compared with £82 in Paris, £54 in New York, and £21 in Brussels (though some London rents had fallen by a quarter by 1975). Even during the rent freeze of 1973–4, many overseas firms were choosing Anglophone Dublin as a European Community base. Once again, London's authorities are schizophrenic: they want to attract certain types of prestige office tenants, but they also want to reduce pressure on the centre by displacing the office workforce. There are other ways, of course, to combat the rush hours, by 'flexitime' working and the introduction of a four-day working week, but the adoption rate for these novelties is low.

Seeking a balance

Because this volume is in a series about problem regions, the narrative has concentrated on problems. Certainly problems abound in London and its region, as an annual stream of reports by commissions, committees, and individuals testifies. But that is only part of the annual outpouring of Londiniana. Artists choose to select some enduring visual charms of London and writers eulogize the continuing excitement of its sometimes abrasive cosmopolitan life. Despite the unceasing struggle to improve the conditions of London life and labour and to eliminate the hardships of the London poor—old people trapped in the inner city or younger people forced to commute from the Outer Metropolitan Area—the excitement and variety of metropolitan living outweighs the problems for many residents, commuters, and visitors.

London's corporate task, the task of the G.L.C., the boroughs, and the public and private firms whose investments of money and effort drive the metropolis, is to keep the balance positive. For some this implies avoiding the disproportionate squeezing out of middle-income and middle-age groups, or keeping a scale more suited to the pedestrian in wind and rain than the businessman looking for landmarks from an aircraft window more than 500 m above the City.

One persistent hindrance to the gradual transition of London from an empire's congested capital of 8·6 million people to a world city of 2 million fewer people in a South East region close to the European economic heartland, is the artificial boundary of the G.L.C. and of the Green Belt which reinforces its insularity. Both the Layfield *G.L.D.P.* inquiry panel and the Town and Country Planning Association see virtue in a reduced population within the G.L.C. area. Rehousing need not be of such high density, congestion may be reduced, and so on. But the G.L.C. reacts with dismay rather than satisfaction. Why should London ratepayers, it is argued, subsidize transport services and street cleansing which also benefit commuters and tourists from beyond the G.L.C. boundary? Perhaps the new Layfield Committee's examination of local authority finance will result in better ways being found to support the income of cities like London which are losing population and jobs from within their political and administrative boundaries to neighbouring authorities.

No other planning region in Britain, and few elsewhere in Europe, are so dominated by the central urban mass. Planning for the restructuring of the metropolis and the channelling of growth in the South East region continues to be confused and confounded by the mixture of statistical, political, and financial viewpoints which prevents a regional conspectus developing. Perhaps such a view will never prevail except in planners' minds or reports. Meanwhile Greater London faces urgent tasks and moulds new policies into programmes. So far the effort has enabled London and the South East to maintain a dual status. It is, to be sure, one of Europe's problem regions, but it is also one of Europe's prime regions of cultural, educational, and economic opportunity, and of visual and historic attraction.

Further Work

Ideally, visual investigation—by foot or from the top deck of a bus—should augment any documentary analysis of London's problems. A visit to central London should include the new Museum of London and also either of the G.L.C. bookshops (54 Charing Cross Road, WC2 or at the County Hall, SE1). From the range of material listed in the G.L.C. *Publications Catalogue*, the *Greater London Intelligence Quarterly*, *Annual Abstract of Greater London Statistics*, and *Research Memoranda* are particularly useful.

Two sheets of the Ordnance Survey 1:50 000 Second Series cover Greater London: 176 (West London) and 177 (East London). Most of the wider region appears on the 1:250 000 Sheet 17 (South East England). There are two atlases of London: J. Shepherd, J. Westaway, and T. Lee's *A Social Atlas of London* (Clarendon Press, Oxford, 1974) is compact; the 70 sheets in the *Atlas of London and the London Region* edited by E. Jones and D. J. Sinclair (Pergamon Press, Oxford, 1968–9) are more bulky.

Metropolitan society past and present is reviewed in *The London Journal*, and topical comment appears in *Time Out*, London's two newspapers (*Evening News* and *Evening Standard*), and local radio broadcasting stations. The struggle to civilize the metropolis is illustrated in F. Barker and P. Jackson's *London: 2000 years of a city and its people* (Cassell, 1974).

Selected further reading

General works

DONNISON, D. and EVERSLEY, D. (eds.), *London: Urban Patterns, Problems and Policies* (Heinemann, 1973).

HALL, P., *London 2000* (Faber and Faber, 2nd edition, 1969).

London government and plans

ROYAL COMMISSION ON LOCAL GOVERNMENT IN GREATER LONDON 1957–60 (Chairman: Sir Edwin Herbert), *Report and Maps* (Cmd. 1164, H.M.S.O., 1960).

RHODES, G., *The Government of London: the Struggle for Reform* (Weidenfeld and Nicolson, 1970).

DEPARTMENT OF THE ENVIRONMENT, *Greater London Development Plan: Report of the Panel of Inquiry* (Chairman: Frank Layfield, Q.C.), 2 vols. (H.M.S.O., 1973).

GREATER LONDON COUNCIL, *Modified Greater London Development Plan* (G.L.C., 1975).

LONDON DOCKLAND STUDY TEAM, *Docklands: Redevelopment Proposals for East London*, 2 vols. (G.L.C., 1973).

EXPENDITURE COMMITTEE (ENVIRONMENT SUB-COMMITTEE), *Redevelopment of the London Docklands* (H.C. Paper 348 Session 1974–5, H.M.S.O., 1975).

Redevelopment of the London Docklands (Cmnd. 6193, H.M.S.O., 1975).

COVENT GARDEN DEVELOPMENT TEAM, *Covent Garden Local Plan: Report of Survey; Discussion Papers*, 1–6 (G.L.C., 1974).

City and region

GODDARD, J. B., *Office Location in Urban and Regional Development* (Oxford University Press, 1975).

The Dispersal of Government Work from London: Statement by the Government, and *Report* by Sir Henry Hardman (Cmnd. 5322, H.M.S.O., 1973).

HALL, P., 'London's western fringes', in HALL, P. and others, *The Containment of Urban England*, vol. 1 *Urban and Metropolitan Processes, or Megalopolis Denied* (Allen and Unwin, 1973).

THOMAS, D., *London's Green Belt* (Faber and Faber, 1970).

THOMAS, R., *London's New Towns: a Study of Self-contained and Balanced Communities* (Political and Economic Planning, Broadsheet 510, 1969).

The changing metropolis

LOMAS, G., *The Inner City* (London Council of Social Service, 1975).

YOUNG, M. and WILLMOTT, P., *The Symmetrical Family: a Study of Work and Leisure in the London Region* (Routledge and Kegan Paul, 1973).

COUNTER INFORMATION SERVICES, *The Recurrent Crisis of London: C.I.S. Anti-Report on the Property Developers* (C.I.S., 1972).

HOBHOUSE, H., *Lost London* (Macmillan, 1971).